learning
to live
without
violence

Has highlighting
in book. 9/4/91
SB.

D0564544

HV 6626 .S65 1989

Sonkin, Daniel Jay.

Learning to live without
violence

AMERICAN RIVER COLLEGE LIBRARY
4700 College Oak Drive
Sacramento, California 95841

learning to live without violence

A HANDBOOK FOR MEN

by Daniel Jay Sonkin, Ph.D.
and Michael Durphy, M.D.

VOLCANO
PRESS

Copyright © 1982, 1985, 1989 by Daniel Jay Sonkin and Michael Durphy

All Rights Reserved. No part of this book may be copied or reproduced by any means without prior written permission of the publisher.

First printing, Volcano Press, Inc., 1982

Printed in the United States of America.

Library of Congress Cataloging-in-Publication Data
Sonkin, Daniel Jay.
    Learning to live without violence.
    Bibliography:
    1. Wife abuse–United States–Prevention. 2. Men–
Counseling of–United States 3. Violence–United States–
Psychological aspects. I. Title.
HV6626.S65   1989   362.8'3   88-33926
ISBN 0-912078-84-7 (pbk.)

Volcano Press participates in the Cataloging in Publication program of the Library of Congress. However, in our opinion, the data provided us above by CIP for this book does not adequately nor accurately reflect the book's scope and content. Therefore, we are offering our librarian and bookstore users the choice between CIP's treatment and an Alternative CIP prepared by Sanford Berman, Head Cataloger at Hennepin County Library, Edina, Minnesota.

Alternative Cataloging-in-Publication Data
Sonkin, Daniel Jay.
Learning to live without violence: a handbook for men. By Daniel Jay Sonkin and Michael Durphy.
Updated, expanded edition. Volcano, CA: Volcano Press copyright © 1989.
PARTIAL CONTENTS: The men, women, and children. -Anger management. -Alcohol, other drugs and violence. -Feelings and communication. -Becoming an assertive man. -Stress reduction. -Changing patterns with your partner. -What if she leaves?
1. Family violence–Prevention. 2. Woman battering–Prevention. 3. Woman batterers' services.
4 Violence in men–Prevention. 5. Stress management for men. 6. Woman batterers–Psychotherapy.
7. Letting go (Psychology). 8. Anger in men–Control. 9. Assertiveness training for men. I. Volcano Press. II. Durphy, Michael. III. Title. IV. Title: Living without violence: a handbook for men.
V. Without violence: a handbook for men.
362.882

The following sources are acknowledged with thanks:

The National Council of Alcoholism for permission to use the questionnaire in Chapter 9.

Susan King, Co-Alcoholism Trainer, for permission to use the questionnaire in Chapter 9.

Cover Design: Wolfgang Lederer

Computerized Laser Typesetting: Crosby Associates, P.O. Box 248, Sutter Creek, CA. 95685

Please enclose $11.95 for each copy of *Learning to Live Without Violence* ordered. For postage and handling, add $3.00 for the first book and $.75 for each additional book. California residents please add appropriate sales tax. Please contact Volcano Press for group discount prices.

Volcano Press, Inc., P.O. Box 270, Volcano, CA   95689   (209) 296-3445   Fax: (209) 296-4515

Of additional interest from Volcano Press:

Battered Wives, by Del Martin $10.00 paper

CONTENTS

All of the cases and examples presented in this book were taken from patient material. In each case, the names, locations and identifying details have been changed. In some examples, we created a composite of several patients' stories.

Acknowledgements

The total list of people who have in some way influenced the development of this book is too long to mention. However, a number of persons and agencies should be acknowledged because of their special contributions.

We would like to thank the entire staff of the Family Violence Project of the San Francisco District Attorney's Office for their encouragement, feedback and generous support of the reproduction and distribution of the first draft of this workbook. Their commitment to addressing family violence in San Francisco serves as an example and inspiration to programs across the country.

Anne Ganley and Lance Harris of the American Lake Veterans Hospital in Tacoma, Washington were two of the early pioneers in working with men who batter. Their use of anger management material (Time-Outs and Anger Journal) in their groups helped to form the basis of our work.

Del Martin (**Battered Wives**, Volcano Press) is considered the founder of the modern day battered women's movement in this country. It was Del who showed an early draft of this book to Volcano Press, which ultimately led to its being published in its current form. Thank you, Del.

Lenore Walker, of Denver, Colorado, is another leader in the movement. Her contributions have influenced mental health professionals and social advocates around the world to address this crucial issue. Her continued support of our work is greatly appreciated.

Jon Mitchell of the Adolescent Recovery Center at Marin General Hospital in Greenbrae, California for his helpful feedback and thoughts about chemical dependency.

This book would not have been possible without the support and influence of the many women and men of the battered women's movement, without whose devotion, persistence and skills battered women, children, and batterers would not be receiving the services they greatly need.

We would also like to thank our publisher, Ruth Gottstein, for her guidance in preparing this book, and her commitment to ending violence against women.

And last, but not least, thanks to the many men who came to us seeking to *Learn to Live Without Violence*.

Daniel Jay Sonkin

    &

Michael Durphy

Marin County, California, 1989

INTRODUCTION TO THE THIRD EDITION

Learning to Live Without Violence is for men who are currently in counseling for violence, men who are violent but not yet in counseling, or men who are not yet violent but are fearful that they may become violent. This updated edition is the result of six years of using it in our groups. We have incorporated changes suggested by men and counselors who used the earlier editions, and have further developed some issues, rearranged some chapters, and added a great deal of new material. Whether this book is new to you, or you have already used an earlier edition in a program or by yourself, we know that it will be useful.

Learning to Live Without Violence is written in workbook form, so that you can immediately begin to change behavior by completing the exercises and homework. At the end of each chapter there are questions to help your understanding of the material. We encourage you to take your time and complete the exercises as they are prescribed. **Follow the instructions carefully.** Although your impulse may be to "get through as soon as possible," changing your patterns will take time and constant awareness.

We know that men can and do change their behavior with the help of this book. However, *Learning to Live Without Violence* is **not** intended to replace professional counseling. It is our firm belief that in order to ensure ending violence in a intimate relationship, the person doing the battering needs weekly counseling for a period of time. After the violence has stopped, and if the couple wants to stay together, couples' counseling may be part of the plan. If you are looking for counseling now, please read Chapter 13 first, which discusses how to find a counselor.

Although ten years ago a batterer had a hard time finding appropriate help, today this is not the case. There are more counseling programs for male batterers, including court-mandated ones, improved police training on this issue, and better understanding of the issue by counselors. You don't have to solve this problem by yourself. The costs are too high — to your partner, your children — and yourself. We have found that the more support a man can get, the more likely he is to use the material in this book on a regular basis.

No one likes to confront a side of himself of which he is not particularly proud, and you may find all kinds of reason to let this work slide. One client put it well when he told us, "It is like when you take antibiotics for an infection. After two or three days you're feeling great, so you stop taking them for the full ten days. If you stop, the illness returns and you are back to square one. We all need to take the full dose and not be lulled into a false sense of security just because we are feeling better."

We hope that you find the inner strength to make this journey from beginning to end. The road may not always be easy, and you will certainly feel like giving up at times. But we can guarantee that finishing the journey will be rewarding to you and your family.

You **can** live your life without violence.

Daniel Sonkin & Michael Durphy

A Note to our Colleagues

We have learned over a number of years, and from many clients, that domestic violence is a potentially lethal situation that must be dealt with directly by both client and counselor. Our experience, and that of many other counselors in this field, has shown that a style of counseling which focuses on anger management, communication, education about sex role attitudes, power and control in relationships and self-esteem building has proven to be most effective in helping men to eliminate family violence from their lives.

Most professional training has traditionally omitted theoretical and practical work in the field of domestic violence. If this is the case for you, we encourage you to read other books on this topic (EMERGE, 1981; Ganley, 1981; Martin, 1981; Walker, 1979; 1984; Sonkin, Martin & Walker, 1985; Sonkin, 1987, Sonkin, 1989) so that you may have a better understanding of this problem. You may also wish to purchase a copy of this book as a tool for you to use with your clients.

Daniel Sonkin has recently completed several books on this topic. *The Male Batterer: A Treatment Approach* develops a more complete understanding of the psychology of the battering situation and elaborates specific counseling issues and techniques. *Domestic Violence on Trial* discusses the interface between the mental health profession and the courts as it relates to domestic violence. *Wounded Men: Healing from childhood abuse*, helps men recover from their experiences of childhood abuse.

We would like to reiterate that incidents of domestic violence have a very high frequency of serious injury and death. This is why we say, "Stop the violence first," then work on underlying psychological issues that may have predisposed the man to violence.

Should you have an experience you would like to share with us, or need additional information on this issue, feel free to contact the battered women's shelter or program in your area, or write to us at the following address:

Daniel Sonkin, Ph.D.

        &

Michael Durphy, M.D.

Volcano Press, Inc.
P.O. Box 270
Volcano CA 95689

(209) 296-3445
Fax: (209) 296-4515

CHAPTER ONE

LEARNING TO LIVE WITHOUT VIOLENCE: AN INTRODUCTION

Domestic violence affects men and women of all ages, races, religions and incomes. It is estimated that approximately three million American households experience at least one domestic violence episode each year. Victims of violence may be spouses, children, or the elderly.

Research has shown that when violence occurs between adults in the family, women and men are equally likely to be the victim; however, because of differences in strength, it is women who suffer the most serious injuries. It has also been found that when women do act violently, it is usually in response to their being abused for a period of time. Women are more likely be violent in self-defense, whereas men may attribute their violence to "controlling their partner's behavior."

In addition to violence between intimate adults, some parents are abused by children, or violence may occur between siblings. This workbook will mainly focus on spouse abuse, although many of the techniques discussed in this book can be applied to other types of domestic violence.

Spouse abuse in any form is very dangerous. It is estimated that between 25% and 30% of homicides are domestic in nature. When a domestic homicide occurs between a husband and wife, the chances are equal that either one can be the victim. However, one study showed that women murder their husbands in self-defense seven times more often than men murder their wives in self-defense.

In 70-80% of the battering incidents, the batterer (and sometimes the battered woman) is under the influence of alcohol or other drugs. Drugs do not actually cause the violence, but may be a factor in creating an argument or conflict situation. When the batterer is under the influence of alcohol or other drugs at the time of the violence, he is likely to commit more serious violence that may lead to injuries requiring medical care.

In over one-third of families where spouse abuse is a problem, child abuse also occurs. This abuse may be physical or sexual and either parent may be the abuser. In families where there are children, the children have either witnessed the violence between their parents or are aware of its occurrence. It is estimated that over three million children witness family violence each year. Many children try to stop the violence between their parents, only to suffer injuries themselves. Many children are injured when the violence between the parents spills over on them. However, whether a child is directly abused or not, studies show that children who grow up in homes where there is domestic violence often develop serious emotional problems later in life.

Over sixty-five percent of the men in our program saw their fathers abusing their mothers or were themselves victims of child abuse. This tells us one way violence affects the children. Boys learn that violence is an acceptable way of dealing with anger, frustration and stress. Girls learn that they must live with it. Violence also affects children before birth. It is estimated that one-fourth of all women who are abused are struck during pregnancy. Many of these women miscarry as a result of the violence.

Spouse abuse doesn't only affect the family involved. Police officers responding to domestic violence calls are often injured. Family members or neighbors who try to intervene may also get hurt. Women miss work because of injuries, men miss work because of arrests. Sometimes people lose their jobs. Many times women need medical care, which costs money. If medical insurance is used, rates subsequently increase. If the court is involved, there are attorneys' fees and more work absenteeism. Children often get caught between their mother and father; in-laws may get involved and tension between family members increases.

As you can see, spouse abuse is a prevalent and serious problem in this society. We hope that by reading this far you have already made the decision to stop your violence now!

What is Violence?

When men come into our group they quickly learn that everyone has a different definition of the word "violence." Some men feel that a slap or a shove is not being violent, while other men think that any angry physical contact can be considered violence. You probably have different definitions of domestic violence than your neighbor or the man sitting next to you in your group. We believe that in order for everyone to understand each other when we use words such as "violence," we need to have a definition that each person can begin with.

Our definition may be different than yours, but at least you will know what we are talking about throughout this book. So, according to Webster's Dictionary:

Violence: Exerting physical force so as to injure or abuse

This definition is good, but not quite complete for our purposes. When we speak about domestic violence, we can be talking about three different types of violence. They are:

1. Physical violence

2. Sexual violence

3. Psychological violence

Let's now try to clearly define each of these types.

Physical Violence

Physical violence is probably what comes to most people's minds when we talk about domestic violence. This includes: hitting, slapping, grabbing, shoving, pushing, kicking, choking, scratching, punching, pulling, hitting with weapons or objects, physical force to make a person do something or go somewhere against that person's will. "She slaps me in the face, is that violence?" **Yes.** No one is justified in using violence except in self-defense. Even then, it takes considerably less force to get away from someone than to engage in a fight, retaliate, or try to teach someone a lesson.

2

Sexual Violence

When someone forces another person to have sexual intercourse by means of physical force, the threat of force, or by use of a weapon, it is considered rape. And that is one form of sexual violence. Sexual violence is not something that occurs only between strangers. In fact, a good number of rapes occur between individuals who know each other. Other forms include forced sexual activity (oral sex, sodomy, etc.), forced sex with animals, forcing a person to have sexual intercourse or sexual activity with another person, or forced sexual activity with objects. In many states, it is now against the law for a man to force his wife to have sex with him. It is called spousal rape, and has already been tested successfully in the courts.

Psychological Violence

This can be expressed several ways, but essentially it is a systematic attempt to control another person's thinking and behavior. A man may accomplish this by making either direct or veiled threats of physical violence. He may combine these threats with occasional violent acts as a means of keeping his partner constantly intimidated. When she is paralyzed with fear, he can feel in control. Violent threats and actions may be aimed indirectly at a partner, through destruction of property or pets. If she is watching him break up furniture or dishes, or punch a hole in the door, she is likely to feel frightened and insecure — and willing to agree with him to get him to stop.

The aim of this psychological violence is to damage the victim's sense of self-worth, to make her feel powerless. She has to give up her own values, her point of view, in order to keep him from being out of control. He may also try to break down her self-esteem by degrading her through name calling, humiliation, and demanding that she always put him first. Because of extreme jealousy or insecurity, he may dictate her every move and accuse her of things she could not possibly have done. This may get to the point of trying to isolate her at home, with minimal or even no outside social contacts.

The outcome of this is similar to the "hostage syndrome," in which the captive becomes emotionally dependent on the captor. Because he controls her every action, she may come to feel she can't survive without him, and may grow even more dependent. In the short run, this may be what he wants. In the long run, though, psychological violence, like physical and sexual violence, almost always destroys the relationship.

What to they have in common?

These three types of violence have several other characteristics in common.

First, they are all **against the law**. Physically or sexually assaulting someone, threatening to assault or kill another person or destroying another person's property are all against the law.

Second, they each can have serious emotional or physical consequences for the victim, unintended victims such as children, and the offender himself.

Third, they are ways in which someone can dominate, control and intimidate another person.

3

Lastly, any type of violence is only one way of dealing with anger, conflict and disagreement in a relationship. There are other ways; this is what *Learning to Live Without Violence* is all about!

Your Violence History

When a man enters counseling, he is likely to be asked, "What type of violence have you perpetrated?" Admitting to violence is going to be difficult for you. You are likely to feel embarrassed, shameful and afraid of other people's response to you. Acknowledging your violence forces you to look at a part of yourself of which you are not particularly proud. But this honest acknowledgement will ultimately help you to change those behavior patterns that are likely to lead to violence.

What types of **physical violence** have you perpetrated in the past? What was the worst incident? What was the first incident? What was the last incident? Be specific!

What types of **sexual violence** have you perpetrated in the past? Be specific!

What types of **psychological violence** have you perpetrated in the past? Be specific!

How to stop the violence — NOW!

The Time-Out is a guaranteed method for stopping the violence from now on. This method has been successfully used by many men who have attended our program. All it takes is your conscientious effort to do this exercise faithfully.

Time-Out: Whenever you feel your anger rising, your body getting tense as if it is going to explode, or you begin to feel frustrated or out of control, say out loud to yourself and your wife or lover:

"I'm beginning to feel angry and I need to take a Time-Out."

Leave your home for one hour (no longer and no shorter), during which you cannot drink and you should not drive (unless it is absolutely necessary). It is most preferable for you to go for a walk or run, to do something physical. If you begin to think about the situation that made you angry, just say to yourself: "I'm beginning to feel angry and I need to take a Time-Out." In this way you will be taking a **mental** Time-Out as well as a **physical** Time-Out.

When you return in one hour, check in and tell your partner that you have come back from your Time-Out and ask if she would like to talk with you. If you **both** want to discuss the situation, tell her what it was that made you feel angry. You may also want to talk about what it was like for you to take a Time-Out. If one of you doesn't want to talk about the situation, respect that person's need to not discuss it. In either case, if you find yourself feeling angry again, take another Time-Out.

Some topics of conversation may be too charged to talk about. If this is true in your situation, put that issue on the shelf for a while, acknowledging that it is too difficult for the two of you to discuss alone. Take these issues and others to a counselor to get some help working them out. Even if it's an important issue that is making you angry, think of your priorities. Nothing can be more important than stopping the violence!

How Time-Outs Work

Let's now look at the different aspects of the Time-Out to see how and why it works.

I'm...

An "I" statement. You begin by talking about yourself, and talking about yourself immediately puts you in charge of yourself. You aren't name-calling or blaming.

Beginning To Feel Angry...

You are talking about how you feel. It's a direct communication.

Nothing unclear about this statement. Saying you feel angry may in fact make you feel **less** angry. Try it — you'll like it!

I Need To Take A Time-Out.

Another "I" statement. You are also saying to your partner that you are not going to hit her; instead, you're going to do something else, take a Time-Out. Taking a Time-Out helps build up trust with the other person — that in fact there will be no violence.

Leave For An Hour...

If you stay away for the full hour, you and she should be sufficiently cooled off by the time you return.

Don't Drink, Use Drugs Or Drive...

Drinking and drugs will only make the situation worse. Don't drive because there are already enough angry people on the roads!

Do Something Physical...

Going for a walk, a run or a ride on your bicycle will help discharge some of the angry tension in your body.

Come Back In An Hour — No Sooner — No Later...

If you agree to come back in an hour, live up to your agreement. It helps to build trust. In addition, an hour will give you enough time to cool off.

Check In — Talk About What It Was That Made You Angry...

If you do no more than check in, you completed the exercise. If you go on to talk about what it was that made you angry, you get experience and practice in communicating and discussing emotional issues.

When there has been violence in a relationship, the trust factor drops significantly. This Time-Out exercise not only helps to stop the violence, but also helps to rebuild trust. Trust takes some time to rebuild. Just because you may take one or two Time-Outs, it doesn't mean that everything is OK. Be patient! Concentrate on identifying your anger and taking your Time-Outs. The rest takes time.

IMPORTANT!

Be sure to tell your wife or lover about the Time-Out and how it works. You might even want to read this chapter aloud and talk about it together. No matter which way you do it, be sure she understands what the Time-Out is, how and why it works.

Time-Outs are hard to do!

Why? Because men grow up to believe that only a coward will walk away from a fight. Your impulse will be to stay and finish it, or at least get in the last word. But, think of what is most important to you. Is it more important to maintain your image as a "real man", or to stop the violence?

Many men have also expressed the fear that their partners will be gone when they return. This is part of the trust building; as each of you follows through with your part in taking a Time-Out, the trust will grow.

The other frequent problem men have with Time-Outs is staying away from alcohol. Many people use alcohol to treat loneliness, and you may feel quite alone during your Time-Out. Also, men will often go to a bar to hang out with their buddies when they need support or someone to talk to. We want to emphasize again that alcohol can make an argument much worse.

Don't drink or use drugs!

Although taking Time-Outs may be difficult for you initially, they will get easier with time and practice.

Practice Time-Outs

Practice Time-Outs will help you to take your real Time-Outs. What's a practice Time-Out? It's the same as a real Time-Out except for two things: First, in a practice Time-Out you are not feeling angry. Second, the practice Time-Out is only half an hour. It's just practice at saying the words and walking away. You tell your partner:

"I'm NOT beginning to feel angry, but I want to take a Practice Time-Out."

The more you take practice Time-Outs, the easier it will be to take real Time-Outs.

Homework

Take **three practice** Time-Outs and at least **one real** Time-Out when you are feeling irritated, annoyed, angry, or enraged every week while you are working in this book or in your program. Yes, **every week**! And, yes, even when you're just irritated. If you can't take a Time-Out when you **don't** need it, you will probably not take a Time-Out when you **do** need it. In addition, when those little irritations are not communicated and dealt with, they build up to full scale angers and rages. Through weekly practice of the Time-Outs you will find it easier to identify your anger, live with it, and avoid violence.

speak a different language, and they each become frustrated because they do not understand each other.

Many men who batter have strongly fixed ideas about what women and men should be. All of us have ideas of what women and men are "supposed" to be like, which we get from our families and from society as we grow up. But women are feeling more free these days to express themselves **outside** the traditional roles that they've grown up with. Men who are violent toward women are more likely to feel angry and uncomfortable with this change. They hold on to the traditional image of "woman" they carry inside, and tend to demand that their partners act that image. We believe this is related to the issue of self-esteem, as discussed above. A man who is sure of himself, confident in his self-worth, usually has a much easier time accepting change and growth in intimate relationships.

Men who batter tend to be **isolated;** they do not have close friends with whom they can discuss their problems. Many of them consider themselves "loners." This is why we encourage men to join a domestic violence men's group, so that they can talk about their problems with other men in similar situations, and discover that they are not alone in their feelings.

Men who batter tend to have **explosive tempers**. As you will learn from reading this book, anger erupts violently when a person holds his feelings inside for a long period of time. A pressure cooker effect occurs where feelings can no longer be held in, and the result may be an explosion. Prior to these explosions, men who batter tend to withdraw much of the time. They are afraid of the angry feelings that may lead to violence, or don't know how to express them directly. So they hide them, stuff them deep inside and withdraw. Later in the book we will discuss how to change this pattern.

Men who batter often have **problems with alcohol or other drugs**. If a man already has a problem with his temper or has already been violent, using alcohol or drugs is like playing with a loaded gun.

Many men who batter **feel out of control in their lives**. This feeling may come from growing up in a violent home where they were unable to control or stop the violence. This feeling may also come from being unable to control their own violence. Many men have learned that in order to feel in control of themselves, they have to control others. This is not necessarily so. You can learn to control yourself and feel powerful without infringing on the rights or well-being of others. This is what *Learning to Live Without Violence* is all about: developing a sense of personal power without taking power away from others.

Domestic violence in all its forms dramatically affects each family member. It is helpful for men who want to stop their violence to clearly see how that violence has affected them, their partners and their children. This is not an attempt to rub your nose in your past mistakes; it is meant to help you understand the changes your family members will have to experience as you recover from your problem with violence. These changes come slowly, so be patient! We have found that, as a man noticeably changes his behavior, his family members begin to recover from the effects of violence.

How does violence affect the woman?

She is likely feel a lot of **anger** towards her partner. This may come out in open hostility, but more often in gradual **withdrawal** and loss of love for her partner. She may **no longer trust** his ability to control his violence, and she may become so **afraid** of him, that she cannot tolerate continuing the relationship. Often at this point, she may leave for safety in a battered woman's shelter, seek divorce, or she may demand that he get outside help if they are to continue as a couple. No matter what alternative she chooses, the man must realize that it will take time for her to feel trusting of him again.

Because of the way women learn to feel responsible for the success of relationships, the battered woman will often **blame herself** for her partner's violence and unhappiness. This self-blaming is made worse by the batterer who **also** blames her for his violence and unhappiness. The woman tries to do "the right thing" so **he** doesn't get upset and violent, but she soon discovers that he will become violent no matter what she does. She may be so **frustrated** that she will eventually become **depressed** and feel helpless. The woman may develop **low self-esteem** because of her inability to stop the violence, and also because of his constant criticism, blaming and put-downs. In an attempt to feel some sense of control over this situation, a woman may become violent herself, either in self-defense or as a way of controlling the time and place of the violent episode.

Many women develop **physical problems** like back pain, headaches, menstrual problems and low energy. Some women turn to **alcohol or drugs** as a way of dealing with their frustration, numbing their emotional pain and lessening the stress of living in a violent relationship.

Some women take out their anger by becoming physically or psychologically **abusive** towards their kids or partners. When this happens we find it important that the woman get violence counseling as well as the man. However, experience has shown us that when the man stops his violent behavior, the woman will usually stop her violence, whether it is directed towards the man or the children.

The Cycle Theory of Violence

Lenore Walker, author of *The Battered Woman*, has found from talking with many women and men about their relationships that there is a distinct cycle of violence that many couples experience. Understanding the cycle theory helps us understand why battered women behave the way they do when confronted with a partner's violence. This cycle has three phases.

Phase I: The Tension Building Stage

During this stage there is tension which may be a result of constant arguing or giving each other the silent treatment, or a combination of both. Sometimes there is minor violence. This stage can last anywhere from days to years. A woman is usually aware when tension is building between her and her partner. When a woman has been battered she may be even more sensitive to this tension because she is afraid of "doing the wrong thing." She will try to control the environment so that he won't become violent. Her fear of his violence may make her more quiet than usual, or more compliant. She may even become more nervous and agitated herself. This tension builds and builds to the point of explosion.

Phase II: The Acute Battering Stage

This stage is what we read about in newspapers or police reports. The violence may be punching, kicking, slapping, biting, choking, pushing, broken arms and noses, black eyes or assaults with weapons. The stage can last anywhere from a few minutes to days. The violence stops either because the woman leaves, the police are called, the man realizes what he is doing, or someone needs to be taken to the hospital. After the violence the woman can be feeling any number of intense feelings. She may also initially be in shock and feel numb. Later, as she comes to her senses she is aware of her fear, anger and feelings of helplessness. Many women think about leaving, and some do leave. Some women feel so helpless about escaping the batterer's violence that they may protect themselves by using deadly force. Fortunately, more and more women are seeking relief through the criminal courts and by using separation and divorce, rather than risking their own freedom by taking the law into their own hands.

Phase III: The Calm, Loving, Respite Stage

During this stage the man is usually sorry for what he has done. He is very apologetic. He will buy her flowers and presents, promise her it will never happen again, sometimes beg for forgiveness. The woman usually does forgive him because she wants to believe that it will never happen again, but she knows it will. Understanding the cycle of violence helps us to answer the question — "Why do women stay?" It is this third stage that keeps women from leaving. It is during this time that she feels his love most intensely. There is, however, a very thin line between love and guilt! The man can be very convincing that he will change and never hit her again. This is the man she married, the man she loves to experience. This occasional reinforcement can be a powerful pull for a woman who is afraid of being by herself, admitting failure in her relationship, who fears she doesn't have employable skills, etc. This stage eventually fades and the tension slowly builds again.

There are three important characteristics of this cycle. First, the more times it is completed, the less time it takes to complete. For example, early in the relationship it may have taken a year or two to go through all three stages; now, ten years later, it takes only a month to complete all three phases. It increases in frequency.

Second, the longer the cycle goes uninterrupted, the worse the violence gets. For example, early in the relationship the violence consisted of slapping and pushing; now, ten years later, it has become broken bones or assaults with weapons.

Third, the longer the cycle goes uninterrupted, the shorter the third stage becomes. For example, early in the relationship the man is very sorry, apologetic and swears it will never happen again; now, ten years later, he doesn't even express his remorse, and the tension phase begins immediately after the violence.

Looking at these three characteristics, it is easy to see how a woman's feelings of fear, anger and helplessness increase over time. She never really thoroughly recovers from the shock of one incident of violence before she experiences another shocking incident. The cumulative effects of repeated victimizations can drive a woman to desperation — murder or suicide. Some battered women numb themselves with alcohol and other drugs, some become chronically depressed, some become hyper-active, some turn into stone and just stop feeling altogether.

We find it important for men to try to recognize and understand how their violence has affected their partners. For those men who grew up in abusive families, it is easier to understand what it is like to love someone and also feel desperately afraid of them. One can also understand how you can feel so much rage towards a person who you also love. When someone you have loved betrays you by acting violently, your sense of trust is greatly affected. You are never sure you can trust that person again, yet at the same time you want to trust again, you want to **believe** it will never happen again.

The Effects of Violence on Children

Children are also affected by domestic violence even if they are not direct victims. Most children have told us that even if they never saw the violence, they knew it was occurring. Many of these children felt **helpless, angry, frustrated, distrustful, fearful and confused**. "Why would daddy do this to mommy if he loves her?" These feelings about violence become a barrier to their getting close to their father and mother, and will interfere with their getting close to their partners when they become adults.

Some children try to **intervene in violent episodes** and as a result may be injured themselves. Boys may learn to become **violent** towards their mother when they become older and stronger; girls may become angry at their mother for not protecting them. Girls or boys may become the **parental child** — that is, the person who takes care of the adult responsibilities, while the mother or father is falling apart. Some children take out their frustrations in school or in social relationships by becoming either **aggressive or withdrawn**. At home some children may try to get between their parents and control the violence, while other children may withdraw and try to stay away from home and family activities.

Children may become **unintentional victims** of violence. The father throws a plate across the room and unintentionally hits his child. A battered woman may grab her infant to stop her partner from being violent. A man may batter his partner while she is pregnant which puts the unborn child at risk.

Some parents also take out their anger with each other by **intentionally victimizing** their child. The man will batter the woman and the child, or he will batter her and she will batter the child.

Whether the child is directly victimized, witnesses the violence or only hears about it from its room, this experience is terrifying, confusing and potentially damaging to his or her healthy psychological and intellectual development. It is beyond the scope of this book to suggest specific interventions for children of violent families. However, if you do have children, we highly recommend that you speak with a counselor about the effects the violence has had on them, and what you can do to counteract those effects.

Why do men batter?

This is a question that is frequently asked, and there is no one answer that is true for all men. Each man who uses violence at home has his own reasons for it. His reasons may be simple or complicated. They may be straightforward and practical, or they may be rationalized and aimed at blaming his partner. We believe that none of these reasons justifies the violence, but understanding them and looking at your own background may help you as you work to eliminate violence from your life. Let's look at the various explanations given by both counselors and the men themselves.

The first reason for a man to use violence is because it works! Violence puts a quick stop to an emotional argument or a situation that is getting out of control. It is also an outlet for frustration which may come from the home situation, or from outside the home. Although it is effective in the short run, violence creates a long list of unhappy long-term effects which may begin to appear after the first incident, or may take months or years to surface in the relationship. These may include fear and mistrust, avoiding contact (especially sexual contact), lowered self-esteem for both partners, and, eventually, destruction of the relationship. Why not find an alternative to violence then?

There **are** other ways to stop an argument or regain control, and the purpose of this book is to teach you to use them. Think for a moment right now about alternatives you might have used in your situation; probably you will come up with some of the same things we will suggest to you — like the **Time-Out** — because they are just common sense.

We live in a violent culture. We see this in news stories, TV programs, movies and sports. Violence gets our attention, sells us cars or cigarettes and has an emotional impact upon us. We learn that violence is effective, and we, as men, have to live up to an image that includes violence. So we don't think of alternatives, because we have been **taught** violence.

Men and Violence

Think of what our society tells us about a "real man." A real man always keeps his cool; he is always rational and knows the answer; he never walks away from a fight; he has a successful career and makes a lot of money; a real man is always there to support his family; he is tough and strong; he does not express his feelings; a real man never fails. How many men can live up to this image? Not many. We are all bound to feel backed into a corner at times by these expectations: there is no room in them to make mistakes, to compromise, or, in short, to be **human**.

Even when we're young, boys learn a very different "language" about violence than girls. We are exposed to physical sports and rough and tumble play. These become a means to release tension and anxiety, or, on the other hand, express friendship. Many different feelings may come out through physical contact. This training may make it more likely that we will express frustration or anger or fear through violence.

We also learn that there is a link between violence and men's power over women. Much of the violence we see in movies and television and read about in books is violence by men toward women. The woman who is beaten or raped may be seen as somehow deserving it. Some images even suggest that the woman actually enjoys the assault. Although one may argue that this is only a story to "entertain" us, recent studies are now showing that this "entertainment" actually may give some people "permission" to act this way in their own lives. One researcher has documented that viewing violent pornography actually increases violent behavior for some individuals who may already be predisposed to violence.

13

Power and Control in Relationships

In the world today it is easy to feel powerless. That is because in many ways we **are** powerless over people and things. For example, you don't have control over whether or not it is going to rain today. But you can be prepared by carrying an umbrella if it does rain. Likewise, you don't have any control over whether or not your boss comes into work in a good mood. You could hope for the best and try to make his life as nice as possible by doing your job, but you really can't control whether he is going have a fight with his wife that morning or get caught in a traffic jam on the way to work. It is easy to feel powerless in the world!

So where and how does one develop a sense of power? Most men turn to their home as a place where they can feel "in control." The expression, "A man's home is his castle" doesn't imply that this is where a democracy exists. In fact, the adage means exactly what it says — the man is in charge. However, as much as men still want to live by this creed, fewer and fewer woman are willing to do so themselves. In fact, our experience has shown that men who are the most traditional in values regarding their home and power, tend to hook up with women who are much more "liberated" than one would expect. What does this mean? It means that on some level these men **want** a more liberated woman. They like what they see that is different in women's behavior, but they are not sure what to do with this woman who behaves differently from their traditional expectations.

In the twentieth century, the women's movement has affected every woman in one way or another. Not that every woman is thoroughly liberated from the oppression of men's power over them, but the idea of women's liberation has seeped in. Even the most conservative women are altering their expectations of themselves and men. Likewise, we believe that men have accepted some of these new views of women as well. They may not agree with them or even understand them, but on a deeper level what they find attractive in women is beginning to change. Today men are dating and marrying women they never would have been attracted to ten years ago. Unfortunately, many men get caught in the crossfire of changing expectations.

Joe was only married a week when he realized that his new wife was not always going to agree with him and do what he wanted. When asked what attracted him to her in the first place he said, "her free spirited nature, her ability to communicate and most important, her willingness to speak her mind." Joe is caught between two centuries. On one hand he remembers how his mother would bow down to his father and do every thing he ordered. On the other hand he is surrounded by women who are very different from his mother. His father never taught him how to respond to a woman who wants to meet him on an equal level.

When faced with the discomfort of the unknown, men do what they have learned from their fathers and other male models — they fight for control. Who is going to be king of the mountain? Men are taught that only through control can they reign over the mountain. How do men control? Violence is a very good method of controlling another person. As it was described earlier in this chapter, violence can weaken the victim, render her powerless and in shock. Many men misinterpret their partner's eventual willingness to cooperate as agreement, rather than self-protection or the result of confusion from repeated batterings.

We believe that, on a deep psychological level, men know that their violence controls and helps them to get what they want through force. However, physical battering is not the only way to control a person.

Like physical assaults, men use sexual violence to establish control in a relationship. As we described in Chapter 1, sexual violence may not only include physically forced sexual acts. It may also include coercive sexual acts, sexual put-downs, demanding sex when the women isn't interested and rejecting sex when the woman is interested. Sexual jealousy is another way of controlling a person.

Threats are also a very effective way of controlling. Men threaten to steal children, kill a woman or her family, kill other men, or kill themselves. Psychological violence, in general, is a way of controlling and intimidating another person. Many men tell their partners when they can leave the house and when they must stay at home. Some men actually isolate their partners from others by living in a rural area and then taking the car whenever they go out. Not letting a partner take driving lessons is another method of control. Some women are not allowed to have access to their checking or savings accounts. Sometimes a man will only let his partner leave the house if he escorts her. If she wants to go to the store or to school, he will drop her off and pick her up when she is finished. He may tell her this is an expression of his love and affection. Constantly telling her what to do and how to do it may be another way of controlling her.

Some men will constantly move around so that a partner doesn't have the opportunity to form close relationships with others, such as neighbors, or schoolmates. Some men are threatened by their partner's family. They will make sure they live far away or limit her contact with them if they live in the area. Some men will threaten to hurt members of her family if she tries to leave him.

Another way men attempt to control women is through mental degradation. When this is done on a continual basis, it becomes a form of brainwashing. She may actually become convinced that she needs him, she is nothing without him, that she can't survive on her own, no one else will put up with her, and that she is crazy or stupid.

For some men, jealousy is a major motivator for trying to control their partners. A man may feel her withdrawal from him, which may be due to his violence. The more he batters her, and the more she pulls away, the more he feels threatened and jealous. Some men create all kinds of jealous fantasies to justify their insecure feelings. Later in Chapter 10 we will examine jealousy and what to do about it.

Sexuality and Violence

Sexual violence has been a major concern for many women since they are most frequently the victims of rape and child sexual abuse. As with economic oppression and physical violence, rape is a way in which men can dominate and control women. A recent study of battered women showed that over 50% of these women were forced to have sex with the batterer. Over 80% of the women interviewed described sex with their partner as unpleasant, and of these over one-third said it was unpleasant because the man forced her to have sex when she didn't want it.

Forcing a woman to have sex, either by physical violence, threats, intimidation or even constant complaining, is an illustration of how men believe that they have a right to sex upon demand. Every man tries to control his partner. This becomes a serious problem when your need to control outweighs your respect for her needs. If you are thinking, "I don't try to control my partner!" we encourage you to take a moment and reflect on it. When was the last time you had the final word in a decision that had to be made? When was the last time you thought, "I make the money, I decide how it's going to be spent?" When was the last time you forced your partner to do something against her will? When was the last time you hit or tried to intimidate your partner? When was the last time you told your partner what to do? These are all examples of men trying to control women. Men grow up being taught they have to be in control of themselves, their partners and their families. When they feel their control is being threatened, they resort to violence as a way of regaining that control.

Any oppressed group of people wants to gain respect and power as equals. That is what the women's movement is all about: women wanting equal power on all levels, at home, at work and in government. Women are struggling to change the behavior they were taught, such as being passive and tolerant of abuse, so that they can feel more powerful, self-assured and self-confident. Many men are doing the same. These men are questioning the attitudes they have been taught about what it is to be a man and what to expect from women. If a man truly wants to stop the violence in his life, he has to examine how his attitudes about men and women have contributed to that violence.

Childhood Abuse

In addition to these traditional attitudes that men have learned, some men have had the unfortunate experience of growing up in a home where there was violence. Over two-thirds of the men we have seen in our groups have either been physically or sexually abused as children, or saw their father abuse their mother. Growing up in this environment can be very traumatic for a child, leaving deep wounds that follow him or her throughout life. Men who grew up experiencing violence have learned that violence is one way of dealing with anger, stress and frustration. From a psychological point of view, men who were abused directly or observed a parent being abused probably felt quite helpless to do anything about it at the time. As they grow up, they are determined to not feel helpless again, and as a result may resort to violence. Certainly, violence can make you feel powerful — but at the expense of making others feel powerless. Later in this book you will learn ways of feeling powerful that don't involve taking power away from others.

Men abused as children also grow up feeling a lot of intense anger. It is not unusual for men to unload those feelings onto their family when tempers flare. This accounts for why many male batterers over-react to situations. Not only are they expressing their current feelings about something, but they may unconsciously use this situation to unload old anger that they have been carrying around for many years. Many men abused as children may also turn to alcohol or drugs to numb themselves from the inner pain they experience from being a victim of abuse as a child. In addition to these intense feelings, their own childhood experiences may contribute to harmful attitudes about themselves and relationships. They are often distrustful of others, and as a result fear intimacy. This attitude may be evident in their refusal to express their inner thoughts and feelings, their tendency to withdraw from conflict, their difficulty hearing constructive criticism, or their intolerance of others' feelings.

Men who were abused as children need to get counseling, so that those experiences do not negatively affect their relationships today. It may be valuable for you to discuss your feelings about these experiences at some point with a counselor. This will begin the process of healing those old wounds.

Alcohol, Other Drugs and Violence

Alcohol and other drugs play roles in many domestic violence situations. They do not **cause** violence, but they put a person in a frame of mind where he is apt to be more irritable or less inhibited. Some people use violence when they cannot deal with stress and conflict. Others use alcohol or other drugs when they cannot deal with stress or conflict. Some people use both, and violence is likely to be more severe when a man is under the influence.

When you put violence together with alcohol or other drugs you may have a deadly situation. Chapter 5 deals specifically with this issue. It is our belief that men need to seriously consider completely stopping their use of alcohol and other drugs until their violence is well under control.

Friendships

How many men or women friends do you have? Can you confide in these friends, tell them personal things about yourself, talk about the violence?

Over the years we have found that many of the men we have counseled are isolated. When we speak of isolation we are not just talking about having contact with other people, though some men are literally isolated in this way. We are talking about the quality of contact. For example, when you talk with your friends, do you talk about sports and work? Can you also talk about problems you are having at home, including the violence? As we mentioned earlier, part of the training we receive when we are young is a set of rules on how to relate to friends, especially other men. For example, men are taught that it's a sign of weakness if you talk about problems in the home. As long as its "her fault" and doesn't reflect a problem you may be having, its OK to talk about it.

As a result of this training, men tend to be emotionally isolated in their friendships, especially with other men. Since our emotions may expose our more vulnerable side, we hold back expressing feeling for fear of what that other person may think. In fact, the training is so deep that we may not intend to hold back feelings, we may simply not even think of expressing them. That inner fear of judgment by others may be even stronger when we are feeling shame and guilt about our violence. We still want others to see us living up to our ideal male image. As a result, even our close friends may not get to know us as we really are, and we may be emotionally lonely. This type of emotional isolation causes stress, and stress can increase the risk of conflict and the feeling of not being understood.

For these reasons we counsel men in groups, rather than individually. We have heard over and over again statements such as, "It feels good to know there are other men deal-

17

ing with this problem," or "It really helps to get support from other men who have gone through it and have changed."

Perhaps now you can see how you can know someone for years and still feel isolated. Later in the book we will talk about communication of feelings. This type of communication can actually decrease isolation, which can in turn lead to better feelings about yourself and others.

Exercise

How has violence affected you, your partner and children?

Think for a moment about how the violence has affected you. Write down three changes it has caused in your life.

1._____

2._____

3._____

How has the violence affected your partner? You may have noticed changes in her behavior toward you, or you may even ask her about changes she has noticed in herself. Write down three of these changes.

1._____

2._____

3._____

If you have children, how has the violence affected them?

1._____

2._____

3._____

How has it affected your relationship with your partner?

1._____

2._____

3._____

Violence causes many problems with individuals and relationships. **Non-violence** can make these problems diminish and allow them to gradually be solved.

Study Questions

1. Talk with your group about your responses to the above questions.

2. Which of the characteristics of batterers described in this chapter remind you of yourself?

3. Discuss your childhood experiences with violence.

4. Can you ask your partner about how she thinks your violence has affected her? How could you introduce this topic with her?

5. How can you teach your children about non-violence?

6. How is the Cycle of Violence present in your relationship?

CHAPTER THREE

WHEN SOMEONE TELLS YOU: "YOU HAVE TO GO TO COUNSELING"

Many men who have battered their partner have been told they are **required** to attend counseling. These men are likely to be found in programs in the community that work closely with the criminal justice system, and in programs that are affiliated with the military; that is, the Air Force, Army, Coast Guard, Marines, or Navy.

No matter who it is that is telling you that you have to get counseling, whether it is your partner, a judge or your commanding officer, you are likely to feel angry, frustrated, rebellious or even childlike. When you feel like a child you are likely to act like a child. What does a kid do when he is told to do something he doesn't want to do? He pouts, has a temper tantrum, gets depressed. He acts as though he is being told he is a **bad** person, and sometimes finds ways to get around the task. Sometimes a kid will just refuse to do something even if it is good for him. Every man who has been referred to our program has felt these feelings. It's important to acknowledge them, but it's also important not to stop there.

If you are like most men who are mandated to counseling, you will want to blame someone else for your dilemma: your attorney didn't know how to deal with your case, the judge was out to get you, your commanding officer or first sergeant never really understood you, the system doesn't care about individuals. And of course, let's not forget, if **she** didn't call the police you wouldn't be in this mess in the first place. It is certainly easier to blame others, to see ourselves as victims rather than take complete responsibility for our problems. However, our personal and professional experience shows us that problems are likely to continue until you recognize **your** role in creating the problems. Morally and legally, **you** are responsible for your actions. It was your choice to be violent, and it was that personal choice that led to others saying, "This is not acceptable behavior, and you have to get counseling." Why? Because, violence is against the law. No matter who it is that you're victimizing — your wife, lover, friend, boss or stranger — you are committing the crime of assault and/or battery. Police can and do arrest a person who has assaulted his wife or lover or anyone else. This is true in the military as well as the civilian community.

Domestic Violence is a Crime

When a man is arrested in the civilian community, the district attorney may bring the case to trial and the man may be given some jail time and/or probation. Probation is when the offender needs to check in periodically with a probation officer, so that the court can keep informed of his situation.

Many times in domestic violence cases, this probation includes compulsory counseling for a period of time. We encourage this judicial process. Though some men need jail time to realize their errors, most men will not benefit from jail or probation only. We feel that if people knew how to solve their problems on their own, they wouldn't be in trouble in the first place. Counseling can help provide the knowledge that is necessary if you don't want to repeat the behavior that originally got you in trouble.

When an offender is given probation, we encourage the court to add a mental health requirement to probation so that he is given the opportunity to learn new anger-coping skills. Men are then required to attend counseling as a condition of probation.

In many states, when a person is arrested for certain acts that constitute domestic violence — such as battery, assault or disturbing the peace — that person can be "diverted" out of the criminal justice system into a counseling or education program for a period of time — no less than six months, and no more than two years. The length of time is jointly decided by the court, probation officer and counselor. When the person successfully completes diversion, the arrest charges are dropped and his record is clean. That's the payoff for doing diversion — a clean record.

Not everyone is eligible for diversion. There are strict requirements based on past arrest record. You also need to acknowledge that you do have a problem with anger and violence. If you don't think you have a problem, then diversion is not for you. You can find out from your attorney or public defender if your state has a diversion law.

Domestic Violence and the Military

Recent studies have shown that military families also experience domestic violence. In general, many men in this society learn to feel violent, aggressive and superior to women; but men in the military have the additional experience of being trained to fight in war. Preparing for violence becomes a way of life. In addition to this training process, military personnel and their families experience special stresses that civilian families may not experience.

Violence in Context

There are certain situations where violence is not only legal, but is encouraged when necessary. An example of this is war. When a soldier is on the battlefield, it comes down to his and his fellow soldiers' lives, or the life of the enemy. Soldiers are given military training to defend their position or attack the enemy, and under command will carry out that training. In police work as well, an officer is trained to defend himself or herself in the line of duty. If the occasion calls for it, that officer may be required to utilize deadly force when no other options are available. An officer may have to use violence to effectively subdue a suspect resisting arrest. Although there are grey areas in both of these situations where we might question whether violence was necessary, there is agreement among most people that these situations may sometimes require violence.

In other situations, violence is not legal but is excusable due to the circumstances in which it is used. Self-defense is one such example. In many states the concept of self-defense is clearly defined by the law. For example, if someone slaps you in the face you cannot take a gun and kill him or her. A justifiable act of self-defense must meet several standards. First, there must be an apprehension of danger. Second, this danger must be imminent, or likely to occur soon. Third, you must use like force against like force; i.e., you cannot use force that is likely to cause great harm against force that is **not** likely to cause great harm. And fourth, you must be in a situation where you cannot retreat or escape. It is not self-defense if you provoke someone to act violently so that you can be violent. Often a man will say that he was acting only in self-defense, even though his partner was half his size and he could clearly escape her violence.

In most situations violence is clearly inappropriate, inexcusable and against the law. Woman battering clearly falls into this category. However, we have a dilemma. If we are going to teach some professions, such as military personnel, to use violence in specific situations, what do we do when we find some of these persons using that violence in other situations? The solution is simple in theory, but difficult in practice. If we are going to teach someone to use violence professionally, we have a responsibility to teach that person other skills to use in situations where violence is clearly inappropriate. When the conflict is at home and not on the battlefield, men need to learn other techniques to help them resolve conflict or defend their position.

Our experience in counseling active duty service military personnel tells us that men can learn to distinguish between illegal violence and the appropriate expression of anger. In fact, men who experience healthy, non-violent relationships at home are more likely to perform to their greatest potential on their jobs, in the military as well as elsewhere.

Military and Stress

In addition to violence training, military personnel experience daily stresses that may affect a persons frustration and anger level. These stresses include:

1. Low pay and having family to support.

2. Being separated from immediate family for extended periods of time.

3. Having to change locations frequently.

4. Not being able to reach family during tours of duty.

5. Lifestyle differences in interracial/intercultural marriages.

6. Lack of contact with extended family and relatives.

7. Living abroad in different cultures.

8. Lack of privacy, with the military controlling every move.

9. Working long hours at difficult jobs.

10. The need to exercise control over others of lower rank at work, but that control method does not work at home.

11. Having to take orders at work and not wanting to take them at home.

12. Feeling as if the military doesn't care about you or your family.

These stresses can be very real and difficult to cope with for many active duty personnel. Finding a strategy that is effective in dealing with each of these stresses could take a whole book in itself. However, we can help you with one aspect of these stresses, and that is the anger that results from them. Later in this book we will discuss stress and how you can increase or decrease the stress in your life, depending on how you attempt to cope with the situation. Anger is one reaction to stress. If violence is the way you express that anger, then your stress is going to become worse because of the effects violence will have on you and your family, and the military's response to violence in the home. If you can learn healthy ways of dealing with the anger that results from stress, then you will be better equipped to deal directly with the stress itself.

Military command has decided that domestic violence in all its forms can no longer be ignored, and must be treated by trained personnel. Like alcohol and drug abuse, domestic violence affects morale, readiness and job performance. Family Advocacy personnel in all branches of the service are charged with the responsibility of seeing that domestic violence offenders either receive treatment for this problem, or be evaluated for discharge from the service. Programs for batterers are being started on military installations around the world to teach men non-violent ways of coping with stress and conflict at home.

Compared to the civilian community, service personnel have less of a separation between work and home. The civilian man may be able to take a sick day or vacation day from work to attend court. The military man who is arrested for battering his wife is likely to have his first sergeant or commanding officer know all about the incident. This lack of privacy can have a profound impact on how a person perceives others' involvement in his family life. People with helpful intentions may be perceived as invading personal privacy.

Many military personnel are concerned that if they are identified as having a problem with family violence, this fact may affect their career opportunities in the service. At the time of this writing, there are varying opinions leading to controversy about what affect Family Advocacy has on a person's permanent record. Some believe that if a person is identified as having a problem with family violence and successfully completes treatment, his record will not be blemished, and subsequently his career will continue unaffected. There are others who have found otherwise. Because the military response to family violence is so new, it is really too early to know if career advances are being denied because of identification of this problem.

Post Traumatic Stress Disorder

Another stress found associated with the military is Post Traumatic Stress Disorder (PTSD). This condition has been found with military personnel who have experienced combat. PTSD is very prevalent with Vietnam-era veterans who, for a number of reasons, had great difficulty adjusting both to the combat situations in Vietnam as well as returning home.

Many men and women who served in combat or saw the results of combat came back to the states experiencing major changes in their emotional state. Many were plagued with flashbacks, found themselves acting as if they were still in combat, feeling angry, depressed, suicidal, having nightmares and sleep problems, feeling guilty for surviving, having memory problems and feeling as if they wanted to explode. They needed to somehow reconcile what they had to do to survive in Vietnam, with the negative messages they received back in society for participating in the war in the first place.

In 1979, the President signed the Veterans Health Care Amendment Act. The primary purpose of the program was to provide readjustment counseling to Vietnam-era veterans. Today there are programs across the country that deal specifically with the problem of

PTSD as well as discussing readjustment in general, relationship problems, employment development, and substance abuse issues.

If any of the above characteristics apply to you, we suggest talking to someone who knows about Vietnam readjustment at your local Vietnam Veterans Outreach Center or your local Veterans Administration Hospital.

Military Personnel: What To Do

If violence is a problem in your life, chances are you are not feeling very good about yourself or your relationship with your partner. In addition, the military feels strongly that you should deal with this problem, and it can assist you in getting the help that you need. You can look for help on base or in the civilian community. The main difference is that in the civilian community you will be required to pay for services. In addition, the civilian community program may not be required to notify your base of your problem unless there is a specific policy to do so, or if you re-offend while your are in treatment, or your situation is highly lethal.

If you feel that alcohol or drugs are related to your problem with violence, you may want to start the change process by talking with an alcohol or drug counselor on your base or post. This person will probably also be aware of treatment services in your area for violence. A regional military hospital or a branch clinic on base has mental health professionals on staff who are available to talk with you about your family or job difficulties. A specific domestic violence program, sponsored by your branch of the service, may also be available in your area.

Some personnel turn to a chaplain for guidance and support. This may be a good first step for you. You may want to show that person this book, so that he or she may have a better understanding of this issue.

Each military installation has either a family service center or community service center that is specifically set up to address family problems. These centers have counselors on staff that will either work with you in solving your difficulties or will refer you to the person or agency that is best equipped to help you.

Like the criminal justice system in the civilian community, the military command is now taking domestic violence seriously. This means if the family advocacy representative is aware of the violence at home, you will most likely be required to attend counseling. No one likes to be told what to do; however, we encourage you to use this situation as an opportunity to change the course of your life and your relationship. Counseling can either be a punishment, or an opportunity to feel better about yourself and your family; it all depends on how you use it.

Don't forget, you are not alone. Many men in the military, as in the civilian community, are experiencing violence in their personal lives and are getting help from counselors. This is not a sign of weakness. If you had a medical problem you wouldn't think twice about getting help from a doctor; if you were in a pinch in a combat situation you wouldn't think twice about asking for help from your buddies. Likewise, violence in the home is a tough problem that can have many serious consequences for you and your family members. **Ask for help!**

Make the Best of the Situation

If you are being mandated into counseling, use it to your advantage. You can learn new ways of coping with anger, stress and frustration. Your life can be more peaceful.

Many of the men who came to our counseling program ultimately told us that they were glad they **had** to come, otherwise they never would have "stuck it out." This is why mandated counseling programs were developed — for people who ordinarily wouldn't seek counseling unless they had to. Let's face it; all of us have been forced to do things in our lives that we originally didn't want to do, but eventually, we were glad we did it. You can benefit from counseling, even if you **have** to go.

Study Questions

1. Who is telling you to be in counseling? How are you feeling about it?

2. What are the ways you could undermine your success in the program?

3. What are the advantages of attending counseling? Disadvantages?

4. If you are in the military, what are the stresses in your life that affect your mood?

5. How could you inform your C.O. so that he/she knows that you are making progress in counseling? How can you make this experience easier on yourself?

6. If you have served in combat, how have those experiences affected you today? How could a visit to a Vet center help you with your thoughts and feelings about those experiences?

CHAPTER FOUR

RECOGNIZING AND CONTROLLING ANGER

When men come to us for counseling, we often ask, "Have you ever tried to stop the violence on your own? What did you try?" A response that we frequently hear is, "Yes, I tried to work it out on my own; I tried not to get angry." Men often confuse anger and violence. They sometimes think that anger means violence. There is a difference, however, between anger and violence. Anger is an **emotion**, and violence is a **behavior** that can express that emotion. It is normal and natural that throughout life there will be times when you feel irritated, annoyed, angry or even enraged. Anger tells us when something is "not right" with us. We are upset with something we are doing, hearing or seeing. Like physical pain, anger can be a way our body and mind alert us to the situation around us.

Violence on the other hand, is just one expression of anger. In addition, it has a long list of negative consequences. It may mean losing a relationship or being arrested, and it definitely means not feeling good about yourself afterwards.

There are many ways to deal with anger so that you can get your point across. These ways can feel good to you, your partner and your family. Just trying to hold back your anger most of the time may actually lead to explosive outbursts of violence.

When anger is expressed as it comes up, in a direct non-intimidating manner, there is not the build-up or pressure cooker effect that may lead to an explosion. The problem is that many men do not realize when they are feeling angry. It creeps up on them, and they explode. One reason for this is that many people were taught as children that anger is not a "good" emotion to express. As a result, many people do not pay attention to their own anger — and, if they do, they try to keep it inside.

Because many of us learned to be so intolerant of anger, it often is expressed in unhealthy ways. Violence is one of these ways, but there are others. Remember the last time you did a slow burn at home, or gave your partner the cold shoulder? Do you think she got the message that you were angry? We also often express anger by blaming or trying to make our partner feel inferior. In fact, most of us are very creative about finding indirect ways of expressing our anger.

The first step in learning to control your anger is to recognize when you are feeling it at low levels; that is, in the early stages before it gets more difficult to contain. For most people, the body begins to "feel angry" long before their mind realizes that they **are** angry and what they are angry about. Many men have come into our groups stating that they have to understand why they are feeling angry before they express their feelings. This can be a big mistake. It may take you quite a long time (for some it may take hours, days or even years) before you realize just what it was that you were feeling angry about. In the meantime, if you don't express yourself, you could turn into a walking time bomb. How can we tell that we are angry? Start with your body, it doesn't lie.

What are your **body signals** to anger? Most men feel tension. This tension may be in the chest, the arms, the legs, the forehead, the face, the back of the neck or their stomach. Some men state that they get cold while others may sweat. Your heart may start pounding and you may breathe faster. Some men breathe lighter or slower. You may get a headache or a backache.

Exercise: What Are Your Body Signals To Anger?

Think about a situation recently where you felt angry. Picture the situation in your mind and remember what you were feeling and thinking. How did your body feel at the time? Can you feel any of those body signals right now? List four signals you get when you are feeling angry:

1._____

2._____

3._____

4._____

Usually after our body begins to feel anger signals we begin to **act angry**. This often happens **before** we actually realize that we are **feeling angry**. Some men will get verbally abusive or find blame, others may actually become overly nice and try to please. Some people laugh or become humorous, some become sarcastic. Some men become depressed, withdrawn or quiet. Sometimes people will not follow through with their commitments when they are angry. It is not uncommon for men to act out sexually when they are feeling angry; such as having affairs, visiting prostitutes or demanding sex with their partner as a way of avoiding emotional intimacy. Some will have difficulty sleeping or eating, while others may want to sleep or eat more. Some people use alcohol or drugs when they are angry.

Exercise: Your Anger Behaviors

How do you **behave** when you are feeling angry?

1._____

2._____

3._____

4._____

These body and behavior signals of anger are cues as to when you should be taking your **Time-Outs** with your partner. Many men believe that you take a Time-Out only when you think you may become violent. We suggest that in the early stages of counseling, (the first twelve weeks) you take a Time-Out whenever you feel anger. In this way you will begin to automatically think about walking away before you even get close to losing control.

The Levels of Anger

Anger has various levels of intensity, and you may have different body and behavioral cues to different levels of anger. You may also have different words to describe the various levels of anger. We see these levels of anger as being on a continuous scale from 1 (very low level) to 10 (extremely high level). Over the years we have learned that most men tend to be aware only of higher level angers, the 5 through 10 levels. That's because most of us have become adept at ignoring, or stuffing, those low level angers, the 1 through 4's. One reason for this is that most people don't think of a 1 level as really being anger. Instead, we call it annoyance or irritation. But it **is** anger just the same. In fact, it is those annoyances or irritations that we stuff, that build, and continue to build until we explode for a seemingly silly reason. That silly reason becomes the straw that breaks the camel's back. It is our belief that the better you get at recognizing and expressing low level angers, the less likely you are to explode for little or no reason.

The first step in recognizing these low level angers is to identify them with a label or word. Some of the men in our groups have helped you out a bit; try to add to the list with the words **you** use. Circle the words that are already written if you tend to use those words.

Anger Level:	1-2-3	4-5-6	7-8-9-10
	Bugged	Angry	Enraged
	Irritated	Pissed-off	Furious
	Annoyed	Mad	Exploding
	Bothered	Agitated	Fucked up
	_____	_____	_____
	_____	_____	_____
	_____	_____	_____

As you can see, there are many words to describe different levels of anger. We would like you to take Time-Outs **whenever** you are angry with your partner — even if your anger is low-level. The better you get at walking away, even when you don't need to, the easier it will be for you to walk away when you really need to.

Controlling Anger

Once you recognize that you are feeling anger, how can it be controlled? The first thing to realize is that controlling anger does not necessarily mean suppressing it. In fact you have at least three choices.

You can **stuff it!**

you can **escalate it!**

or you can **direct it!**

Let's discuss each one in more detail.

Stuffing

"Stuffing" is very common. It often begins with an "I" statement, but instead of being a statement of your own feelings, it avoids feeling by denial, sympathy, low self-esteem thoughts, blaming or doubting yourself, or intellectualizing. We'll give you an example of each.

Denial . . . . I'm not angry or upset.

Sympathy . . . . She doesn't really mean to get me upset.

Low self-esteem thoughts . . I really screwed up this time.

Doubting yourself . . . . I really don't have a right to get angry.

Intellectualizing . . . . . She's just trying to get me angry. I'm not going to get angry.

Stuffers usually become withdrawn or depressed. But eventually the pressure cooker heats up and you reach a point when you can't stuff anymore and you **EXPLODE!**

Escalating

"Escalating" is easy to identify. Escalators begin their sentences with "You." They may also ask questions such as: "Why did **you** do that?" They blame: "**You** made me angry...It's all **your** fault!" And they call names: "You bitch!" "You ass!" Escalators, in an argument, will increase their anger and may ultimately become violent. Escalation is anything that you do that makes you more angry rather than less angry. For some men, escalation may involve their obsessing about the situation that made them angry. For others, it may consist of trying to get the angry thoughts out of their mind.

Direct It

"Directing it" has a simple formula but in spite of that, it is the most difficult to do. We are not sure why; it may be because we are usually taught as children to stuff and escalate. The formula is two sentences:

I feel angry that _____

I would like _____

Each sentence is completed to make as clear and concise a statement as possible.

Examples:

I feel angry **that you came home late tonight.**

I would like **you to call me if you are going to be late.**

I feel angry **that you yelled at me at the restaurant.**

I would like **you to wait until we leave or talk in a softer voice.**

I feel angry **that you expected me to take care of the kids today.**

I would like **you to tell me ahead of time when you want me to watch them.**

People who communicate their anger directly get their point across, but they also feel more intimate because they communicate in a way that allows direct personal contact with their partner.

At this point you may realize that there have been times you have probably stuffed, escalated and directed or have done any combination of the three. The more aware you become of what you actually do with your anger, the more control you have over how you will express it in the future.

The lottery prize that turned into disaster

Bill can't wait to get home to tell Karen, his wife, that he just won $1000 in the California lottery. Money has been very tight lately, and he needs to repair the car. He tried to fix it himself and it ended running worse that it did before he worked on it. Now he'll need a professional mechanic. He's kept it from Karen because she would have gotten angry at him. She wanted him to take the car to the mechanic in the first place. Now he can afford to get it fixed. Bill walks into the door excited:

Bill: Karen, I won a thousand dollars in the lottery today!

Karen: I didn't know you were playing.

Bill: I've been buying tickets a couple of times a week.

Bill (to himself): I can't believe that she is not happy!

Karen (to herself): He will probably want it for his car as usual!

Karen: Well, finally your investment paid off. Now we can pay off one of our credit cards.

Bill: Karen, I was thinking of fixing up the car. Kind of a present to myself.

Karen: I need to put dinner on the table, we can talk about it later.

Bill (to himself): Here we go again. (Bill walks into the bedroom and slams the door.)

Karen: What are you getting so angry about?

Bill: I am not angry!

Karen: Don't tell me you're not angry. I can see it in your face.

Bill: We always have to pay your credit card bills for your clothes. You don't know how to manage your money. I work hard....

Can you imagine where this argument went from here? Possibly a yelling match, possibly some violence.

This may seem familiar to you. An argument that seems to come out of nowhere. But did it? Bill was doing quite a bit of stuffing and, like a pressure cooker, could only stuff so much steam. It escalated when he began to blame Karen, when in fact it had nothing to do with Karen at all. Much of this could have been avoided by Bill just telling Karen what had happened with the car. But even if Bill chose not to tell her about the car, he still had another alternative, and that was to take a Time-Out!

But could he take a Time-Out just before dinner? There are many potentially awkward situations you may find yourself in when an argument begins to escalate. What if you are in a restaurant or in your car on the freeway when you feel angry? In such situations you may need to be creative to take your Time-Out. Perhaps going to the rest room for an extra long time, or stepping out for a breath of air would work. You may want to pull over to the side of the road and walk a few times around the car until you cool down. You may not be able to take a full hour, but take enough time to cool off and get some perspective on the situation.

What situations can you imagine where it would be difficult for you to take a Time-Out? What solutions can you think of ahead of time?

The Time-Out is an example of directing your anger so as to avoid stuffing, escalation and, ultimately, some kind of violence.

Many men ask, "How can I keep my anger from escalating when I'm on my Time-Out?" Anger is something you **can** control by using **Directing** statements to yourself. Don't forget, **Stuffing** and **Escalating** statements are as harmful when you are alone as they are when you are with another person.

A **Directing** statement may go something like this;

> "I'm feeling angry right now and I need to take a Time-Out. I'm in control of what I do. I need to do something physical like take a walk or run to cool down. Maybe I can talk about this later, but right now I need to take a Time-Out so that I don't become violent. If I do cool down, we could probably talk a lot more calmly about this problem, and at the same time I can begin to rebuild trust with my partner."

The act of recognizing and acknowledging to yourself that you are feeling angry will bring your anger level down one notch. Recognizing and choosing a good alternative at that time, like a Time-Out, means that you are taking control of the situation, and in turn taking control of your life.

This kind of directing statement will decrease the tension in your body so that when you return from your Time-Out you will be cooled off. The tension can be further released by doing something physical such as walking or running. It will take a while for the tension to be released, so be patient! You have a whole hour to make sure you have completely cooled off!

Time-Out Activities

Write down four ways in which you can do something physical during a Time-Out or an anger episode. If you think about it now, you will find it easier to choose your options when the time comes.

1._____

2._____

3._____

4._____

Study Questions

1. Discuss with the group your physical and behavioral signs of anger.

2. What kinds of things get you angry? How do you deal with that anger?

3. Give the group an example of when you have stuffed and/or escalated your anger. How might you have directed it instead?

4. Describe a situation when you were angry. Take a look at the Anger Journal on the next page. How would you have completed the Anger Journal for this incident?

5. What words do you use to describe your low, medium and high levels of anger?

6. When would it be most difficult for you to take a Time-Out? How can you take one even so, or what can you do instead?

THE ANGER JOURNAL

The Anger Journal is a powerful tool in helping men become more aware of their anger, how to control it and how to express it. Write down the date and intensity of your anger (1 being low level irritation or annoyance, and 10 being very angry). Don't forget to recognize all the levels in between. Then note your physical and behavioral signs of that anger. Different levels of anger may have different bodily and behavioral signs. What was the situation where you felt this anger? You will discover that you will feel different levels of anger depending on the situation. Did you take a Time-Out? Watch to see if you stuffed, escalated or directed the anger. What type of "I" statements did you make out loud or in your head? What physical activity did you use during your Time-Out to calm yourself down? And lastly, be aware of your alcohol and drug use before and after these situations when you felt anger.

We encourage you to write in it every day. But at the least, try to fill one out completely at least twice a week.

Anger Journal

Date		
Intensity	1 2 3 4 5 6 7 8 9 10	1 2 3 4 5 6 7 8 9 10
Physical Signs		
Behavior Signs		
Situation		
Did you take a Time-Out?	Yes / No Comments	Yes / No Comments
Did you Stuff it, Escalate it, Direct it?	Stuff it / Escalate it Comments / Direct it	Stuff it / Escalate it Comments / Direct it
"I" Statements	I'm feeling	I'm feeling
Physical Activity		
Alcohol or Drug use?	Yes / No Comments	Yes / No Comments

CHAPTER FIVE

ALCOHOL, OTHER DRUGS AND VIOLENCE

Our data indicate that almost all men who batter also use alcohol or other drugs. Of these, over two-thirds become violent while under the influence of these substances. Statistics such as these could lead you to believe that there is a relationship between alcohol and drug use and violence. And in fact, there is a strong relationship. When we first began to work with male batterers, we thought that if a man solved his substance abuse problem, his violence problem would also be solved. We sent men who were addicted to alcohol or other drugs to treatment programs that handled those problems. Many of them contacted us months later saying that they were no longer using those chemicals, but they were still being violent. On the other hand, programs around the country have found when they have tried to treat the violence **without** solving the alcohol or drug problem, men did not have success stopping their violence.

Our experience tells us that men who completely cease their use of alcohol and other drugs are in a better position to stop their violence. Perhaps you ask, "What if I don't have an alcohol or drug problem but just drink occasionally?" If a man drinks or uses and then becomes violent, that in itself, tells him he has a problem with alcohol and drugs. Being able to stop all use for a period of time can also be one way to test whether or not he has a substance abuse problem. However, even the occasional drinker needs to abstain for a period to: 1) determine the role of alcohol and other drugs in his life; and 2) avoid skating on thin ice while learning how to change his behavior. The last thing you need is something that will increase the chance that you'll become violent.

Although there are no conclusive studies indicating that alcohol or other drugs cause violence, a person is certainly less inhibited while under the influence of drugs or alcohol, and may do things that he might not ordinarily do while sober. A man may batter his wife more violently when under the influence. But alcohol or other drugs do not **cause** the violence and cannot be used as an excuse. According the law, intoxication cannot be used as a defense in criminal court. The laws in many states specifically say that even if a person commits an act while under the influence of alcohol or other drugs, he is still responsible for that act. The law assumes that the person using the substance is aware of the possible consequences of being drunk or high, and therefore is responsible for taking the substance in the first place.

Unless you completely abstain from chemical use, you are not likely to stop your violence. What if you can't stop? We encourage you to get an assessment from a qualified chemical dependency counselor to determine if you need separate chemical dependency treatment.

The Vocabulary of Chemical Dependency

Many people make a distinction between alcohol and drugs because one is legal and the other is not. Their logic goes, "...if alcohol is legal, it must not be as physically or psychologically bad for a person as drugs." In addition, many also believe that drugs are addictive substances, and alcohol is not. Webster defines a drug as "...a substance acting on the nervous system, such as a depressant or stimulant, that can cause an addiction." Alcohol sure fits this description. In fact, throughout time, alcohol has been used as a central nervous system depressant to numb a person to pain. We also know that alcohol, even though it's legal, can be quite addictive, and leads to the disease of alcoholism. So according to Webster, alcohol is a drug — both because of its effect on the body and its addictive qualities.

The distinction that people make between alcohol and other drugs seems to be more arbitrary than based in fact. The only difference between alcohol and pot or cocaine is that a person can legally use alcohol after a certain age, whereas drugs are always illegal. However, just because something is legal, doesn't mean that it's good for you. Since alcohol has the same properties as other drugs, we don't make this distinction. Therefore we use the term **chemicals** to describe any mood altering substance (alcohol, pot, cocaine, speed, downers, prescription tranquilizers, etc.) that can be addictive and potentially dangerous to one's physical or emotional health, or the safety and health of others.

The Effects of Chemicals

All types of chemicals are very powerful and potentially dangerous substances that are readily available in this society. They are frequently used, and abused, by men and women of all ages and backgrounds. The unemployed construction worker who is trying to feed his family may turn to chemicals as a way to cope with the shame of not earning a living. The corporation executive who makes over $100,000 a year uses chemicals to cope with the fear that he is not performing up to his boss's expectations, and may lose his job to an up and coming young executive. There are many different types of chemicals that have various physiologic effects on the body, but in general, the abuse of any chemical may have any one or a number of the following consequences.

1) They can all be addictive, either physically or psychologically.

2) They can all be physically damaging to the body and mind.

3) Over time, an addiction will cause a person to compromise his values.

4) Their use may cover up deeper emotional problems.

5) Their use may be a way of running away from feelings.

6) Their use can lead to family or work problems.

7) Their use can lead to problems with the law.

8) Their use can lead to death.

Aside from these general effects, each chemical has its own physical effect on the brain that affects a person's behavior, his violence in particular.

Chemicals and Violence

Since it is a drug, **alcohol** has specific effects on your body and behavior. Alcohol is a depressant, although it may give a person the temporary feeling that he is able to do or say anything. However, all studies have shown that neither mental nor physical abilities are improved, and in fact they get progressively worse as increasing amounts of alcohol are consumed. Because of its depressant effect on the brain, a person under the influence is less in control of his behavior. For example, after drinking, a person responds more slowly stopping his car in an emergency. Or a person may say something insulting to a friend that he definitely would not say when sober. It is understandable that an argument could develop when one or both persons are under the influence. It is also understandable that a person who ordinarily would agree he has no right to hit his partner, might be violent when intoxicated.

Most persons are also less aware of their emotional state when they are under the influence. A man may not know he is angry or sad until it reaches the point that he can no longer hold those feelings in. Other persons who usually repress their emotions may not be able to when they are under the influence. Men who have difficulty facing the personal or professional stresses in their lives are likely to use alcohol in low to moderate amounts as a way to numb themselves to the feelings that may result from those stresses. Think about it for a moment. You have just come home from work with all its daily problems, and you either don't want to or don't know how to deal with your wife and her problems as well. So you have a couple of drinks. It does take the edge off those feelings. It gives you the illusion of calming down. But, if you have a habit of avoiding problems and a history of violence, you might as well be putting bullets in the gun. This pattern of avoiding problems through alcohol can also be a symptom of alcoholism or chemical dependency.

Like alcohol, other drugs such as **marijuana**, **cocaine**, **opiates** (heroin), **amphetamines** (speed), **hallucinogens** (acid) and **barbiturates** (downers) are not known to specifically cause violence, but are likely to put a person in a state of mind where he will be more irritable or agitated. A person on speed may be irritable if others do not match his level of excitement or energy. Or he may become out of touch with reality, fearful and paranoid during his use of this drug. A person who has been on barbiturates may be more agitated when he comes back to reality the next morning. A person on cocaine may become paranoid that someone is "holding out on him" and may be aggressive towards that person. Someone who has become addicted to a drug such as heroin may become violent in order to get more drugs, or during withdrawal.

Marijuana is the second most frequently used drug after alcohol. Like the other drugs described, heavy marijuana users may become violent because they get irritable during withdrawal, or as a response to wanting the drug and not having it available. Marijuana, just like other drugs, makes a person less in touch with his emotions. These feelings are usually "stuffed", and tend to surface at a later time while the person is not under the influence.

All chemicals are toxins and poison the body. People die from overdose, acute physical reactions, or irresponsible behavior while under the influence. More often, users die a lingering death from chronic health problems. These chemicals also poison your mental health. They don't solve problems or take away pain in the long run, even though they can help a person deny his problems in the short run. The more that emotional pain is denied, the more difficult solving his problems become.

Whatever the reason a person uses or whatever the effects it has on his body and mind, the use of any chemicals makes violence a more likely outcome of conflict in a relationship. Therefore, no matter what your drug of choice is, we strongly recommend that a person stop all drug use while attempting to learn to control his violence. If stopping is difficult, you probably have a problem, and it would be helpful to talk with a drug counselor.

Exercise: The Effects of Chemical Use

What affects has your chemical use had on your life? Does it have any of the effects that we've mentioned above on your emotions or behavior? For example: "We fight a lot about my spending money on pot" or "I have become violent" or "I get more easily agitated by family problems" or "I become verbally abusive."

1._____

2._____

3._____

The Stages of Chemical Use

In order to better determine if alcohol or drugs are a problem in your life, it is important to first understand the progression of chemical dependency. Like domestic violence, alcoholism and drug addiction are progressive diseases that have particular characteristics that develop over time. The following model can be used to describe the addiction process to any mood altering chemical(s). This progression generally looks like this:

Experimentation > Moderate Use > Abuse > Dependency > Death

When a person uses alcohol or another drug for the first time, it is called **experimental use.** This type of use may happen once or twice and last for only a very short period of time. After such use, the person decides either that he likes it and wants to continue, or that he doesn't want to use again. This experimentation may occur out of curiosity or peer pressure, but in either case the person decides whether or not he liked the experience. If he didn't like the effects, he will no longer use that substance. However, if he does decide to use again he quickly moves into the second stage of the process, moderate use.

During **moderate use,** a person's use patterns are fairly predictable. He may drink on weekends, in social settings or with dinner. The amount of alcohol or drugs used will vary from person to person. Most important, there are likely to be few or no consequences directly related to his use. His work life and relationships are not directly affected by his use of the substance. However, if there **is** a consequence as a result of his use, a person will be able to recognize that he needs to make a change in his using behavior. Ultimately he is able to control his use so as to avoid additional consequences.

For example, Joe was at a party where he drank more than he could handle. He got into his car and started driving, but before too long he realized that he was unable to drive safely. He pulled over to the side and thought about his options. He could either continue to drive and risk a ticket or an accident, or he could walk to the nearest phone and call a cab. He decided to take the safe route and walk. It was about two miles to the nearest phone. He had already walked half way when it began to rain. Of course he had left his umbrella and coat at home that night. By the time he got home it was nearly four o'clock in the morning. He was soaked, developed a serious cold and was laid up for a week. That experience taught him a lesson. Getting drunk wasn't worth all the hassles. He never drank that much again.

When a person crosses over the line from moderate use to **abuse** he is beginning to depend on the substance for its physiological and psychological effects. A person's body undergoes changes that make him less sensitive to the effects of the substance. In other words, he has to use more to get the same effect. The person continues to use for psychological reasons, such avoiding family or work problems, or hiding from his feelings. During this stage his physical need is becoming greater. There is typically a great deal of denial at this stage — he is convinced that his drinking or using is not a problem, and he can stop whenever he pleases. He uses rationalizations, excuses, and blaming whenever others confront him about his problem. The abuser has difficulty seeing how his use affects those around him. Therefore, he doesn't try to alter his use in spite of the concerns of family members, friends or co-workers. Over time the abuser's use may increase in frequency and amount. Problems will begin to develop in all areas of his life. Interpersonal and work relationships may show signs of stress. He may begin to get in trouble with the law. His previous patterns of work and home life may change for the worse. His health may begin to deteriorate.

As a person continues to use, he will develop physiological and psychological **dependency**. He will be compulsive about using. When he does use he will not be able to control his consumption. He won't be able to have just one drink, one joint or one line of cocaine. He may need to use every day in order to avoid severe withdrawal symptoms. Others may have a pattern of periodic binging separated by a few days, weeks or months of no or low use. This person may appear to have it together, but people he is close to both at home and work will become increasingly aware of how alcohol or drugs are affecting his life.

By this time in the process, the chemically dependent person's life is becoming unmanageable. He may be continually involved with the law, having frequent interpersonal problems — such as violence — and troubles on the job. Problems are beginning to materialize in all areas of his life. Most important, the chemically dependent person is in such denial that he refuses to see the relationship between his use and his problems. He blames others or uses excuses as a way of avoiding responsibility for his problem. In addition to his own problems, the chemically dependent person also affects the lives of other people. This is seen most commonly in violence, driving while under the influence, encouraging others to use and serving as a poor role model for his children. Our friend in the last example would be blaming his wife for not leaving the umbrella in the car, or more likely would have kept on driving in the first place. If he was arrested for drunk driving, he would have been angry at everyone else but himself. He wouldn't have seen the relationship between his drinking and his getting a ticket.

The chemically dependent person may experience severe withdrawal symptoms, such as the DT's, headaches, anxiety, depression and hot flashes. He may develop severe irreversible physical damage to the body, such as lungs, nasal passages, liver, heart, brain and kidneys. Many moderate to severe alcoholics or drug addicts are also seriously malnourished. As use progresses, the person reaches the final stage of chemical dependency,

death. This may occur as a result of an overdose, by mixing chemicals or by getting into an accident.

A person's using pattern develops after that first experimental use. The length of time it takes a person to reach the end of the process will vary. A person may use chemicals for years before becoming chemically dependent, or can show signs of chemical dependency right from the first experience. If you have a family history of alcoholism or drug addiction, you are more susceptible to becoming chemically dependent.

How do you find out if you are becoming chemically dependent? Get an assessment from a qualified chemical dependency counselor. At the end of this chapter are suggestions as to where you can get help.

Exercise: Chemical Use Patterns

Men use chemicals for different reasons. Which of these patterns can you identify in yourself? Bring this exercise to your group, counselor or partner and discuss your answers.

_____ To relax

_____ To fit in the crowd

_____ Because of peer pressure

_____ To better relate to friends or family

_____ To avoid friends or family

_____ To avoid feeling depressed

_____ To avoid feeling angry

_____ To avoid an argument

_____ To escape problems at work

_____ To escape problems at home

_____ To feel better about yourself

_____ To feel better about others

_____ To avoid feeling lonely

_____ To feel like you belong to a group

_____ To have fun

_____ To get high

_____ To get drunk

_____ To go to sleep

_____ To feel more relaxed about having sex

_____ To stuff feelings

_____ Other:_____

_____ Other:_____

_____ Other:_____

Many of these reasons are chemical abuse patterns, therefore it's possible that you are becoming chemically dependent. Now is the time to nip the problem in the bud, before the consequences become more serious. Do you really need to use? If so, get help. If not, stop now so that you can get better control over your behavior. Remember to ask yourself, "Am I willing to go to any length to stop my violence?"

Exercise: Chemical Dependency

The following questionnaire is designed to determine if you or someone you know has a problem with chemicals. If you do find that your suspicions are true about yourself or your partner, get help. Unless this problem is addressed, the chance that violence will contiune is very great. Answer each question with a "yes" or "no".

DO YOU HAVE A CHEMICAL PROBLEM?

1. Do you occasionally use heavily after a disappointment, a quarrel or when the boss gives you a hard time?

2. When you have trouble or feel under pressure, do you always use more heavily than usual?

3. Have you noticed that you are able to handle more alcohol or drugs than you did when you were first using?

4. Did you ever wake up on the "morning after" and discover that you could not remember part of the evening before, even though your friends tell you that you did not "pass out"?

5. When using with other people, do you try to have a little more when others will not know it?

6. Are there certain occasions when you feel uncomfortable if alcohol or drugs are not available?

7. Have you recently noticed that when you begin using, you are in more of a hurry to get the first hit than you used to be?

8. Do you sometimes feel a little guilty about your use?

9. Are you secretly irritated when your family or friends discuss your use?

10. Have you recently noticed an increase in the frequency of your memory "black-outs"?

11. Do you often find that you wish to continue using after your friends say they have had enough?

12. Do you usually have a reason for the occasions when you use heavily?

13. When you are sober, do you often regret things you have done or said while high?

14. Have you tried switching drugs or following different plans for controlling or cutting down on your use?

15. Have you often failed to keep the promises you have made to yourself about controlling or cutting down on your use?

16. Have you ever tried to control your use by making a change in your jobs, or moving to a new location?

17. Do you try to avoid family or close friends while you are using?

18. Are you having an increasing number of financial and work problems?

19. Do more people seem to be treating you unfairly without good reason?

20. Do you eat very little or irregularly when you are using?

21. Do you sometimes have the "shakes" in the morning and find that it helps to have a little drink or a hit?

22. Have you recently noticed that you cannot use as much as you once did?

23. Do you sometimes stay drunk or high for several days at a time?

24. Do you sometimes feel very depressed and wonder whether life is worth living?

25. Sometimes after periods of using, do you see or hear things that aren't there?

26. Do you get terribly frightened after you have been using heavily?

If you answered "yes" to any of the questions, you have some of the symptoms that may indicate alcohol or drug abuse.

Remember, you can recover. Treatment for alcohol and drug abuse is available. For more information, contact your local or nearest office of the National Council on Alcoholism.

Co-Dependency

A co-dependent is someone who is close to, loves, or cares for someone with a chemical dependency problem. This may be a spouse, roommate, relative or close friend. The hallmark of the co-dependent is that he or she continues trying to help the user long after it has become clear that the user does not accept the help. The co-dependent person may use the addict like the addict uses alcohol or other drugs. They will depend on that person to raise their self-esteem, to maintain control and to feel needed. They may be as blind to the user's disease as is the person using.

Co-dependents are usually very much oriented toward helping others, and they try to be supportive and helpful to their abusers. What they find, to their frustration, is that their help is completely ineffective at getting their partners off alcohol or other drugs. In fact, their help may even wind up **supporting** the pattern of abuse. Co-dependents usually have a number of very positive personal qualities, such as loyalty, tenacity, responsibility and careful planning. They also, however, tend to have fairly low feelings of self-worth and try to feel better about themselves by feeling needed by others.

While trying to help, what does the co-dependent do that supports abuse? He or she may repeatedly cover up or make excuses for drug-related behaviors. He or she may try to take over the abuser's responsibilities, or shelter him from situations where alcohol and other drugs are present. A co-dependent may make emotional appeals to the user, or appeal to his sense of guilt. The co-dependent may himself accept guilt (or become a "martyr") for his user's actions, and then turn around and punish him for it. Underlying this behavior is the co-dependent's need to be needed. Just as the user is dependent on the bottle or drug, the co-dependent is dependent on the user. In reality, neither can change their patterns without outside help.

If your partner is refusing to get help for his or her problem, you must understand that you cannot **make** that person stop; you are powerless over the abuser's behavior, but you can take care of yourself and your family. There are counselors available for you to discuss your options. Al-Anon and Nar-Anon are for the family and friends of alcoholics and drug addicts. They can be contacted through your local Alcoholics Anonymous or Narcotics Anonymous chapter. Like the battered woman who cannot stop the batterer's violence, the co-dependent cannot stop the abuser's drinking. However, that person can take care of himself or herself and in doing so may have an effect on the abuser! Although there are no guarantees that taking care of yourself will stop your partner from using, you will at least feel better about yourself, knowing that you are no longer helping that person to cause you pain and grief with his addiction.

Exercise: Co-Dependency

ARE YOU A CO-DEPENDENT?

Have you:

1. Been embarrassed at the behavior of someone you know after he or she uses?

2. Poured out liquor or thrown out drugs to keep someone from using?

3. Felt your behavior was making someone else use?

4. Threatened to leave someone because of too much using?

5. Called work to give an excuse for someone who could not work that day because of high alcohol or drug intake the day/night before?

6. Felt angry that your family was not being taken care of because so much money was being spent on alcohol or drugs?

7. Felt fearful at what would happen to you and/or your children if using continues in your family?

8. Gone looking for someone who you think is out using?

9. Called bars, neighbors, friends, looking for someone you believe to be using?

10. Increased your own alcohol or drug consumption to keep up with someone who is a heavy user?

11. Wanted to move and "start over" as a solution to heavy using?

12. Been revolted by others' using behavior?

13. Been unable to sleep because someone has stayed out late using or not come home at all?

14. Resented the fact that there is heavy drinking or drug use occurring in your family, or with someone close to you?

15. Felt hopeless about an alcohol or drug situation?

16. Felt it was a disgrace to talk about a drinking or drug problem?

17. Cut down on outside activities so that you could keep an eye on someone who's using?

18. Nagged or gotten into quarrels with someone who uses?

19. Felt that if the user would just stop using, everything would be okay?

"Yes" answers to several of these questions indicate that you have a co-dependency problem. For more information, contact your local office of the National Council on Alcoholism, or write to the national office for the center nearest you.

ACA: The Adult Child of an Addict

The ACA is a person who grew up in a family where one or both of the parents or adult caretakers were chemically dependent. Some men who grew up in such families describe the family tone as unpredictable and chaotic, whereas others describe it as controlled and rigid. When one of the parents is actively abusing, the other parent is usually actively trying to control the abuser. This leaves little room for attention to children.

Bob grew up with chemically dependent parents. His father was an alcoholic, and his mother was on tranquilizers to cope with her husband's physical abuse. He was the oldest of six kids. His role was that of the "parental child", and he often took over for his mother who was passed out in bed. His father sometimes stayed away drunk for days, so he would have to be the "substitute husband" and take care of his mother. He worked in the neighborhood so that there was money for food. As Bob describes it,

"...I never had a childhood. As far back as I can remember I never had the opportunity to play with other kids or do other 'child' things. I was too busy taking care of my younger brothers and sisters and my mother. She was totally useless. If my father wasn't beating her, she was stoned — totally out of it. Everybody else's needs came before mine. I guess that's why I got married twice and why both of my wives were alcoholics. I love to take care of everyone else but myself. I'm really just learning to do that."

Adult children of addicts have many of the same feelings about their childhood as children who grew up in violent homes. Men feel angry, confused, have low self-esteem and are likely to repeat their parents' patterns of abuse or to find themselves in an intimate relationship with an abuser.

Chemical dependency is called the disease of denial. The behavior is denied and the family members' feelings about it are denied. Roger grew up with an alcoholic mother. He describes the denial in his family:

> "Whenever mom was drunk we would literally ignore her. No one would talk with her or look at her. She became invisible to everybody in the family. We got really good at making up stories about why she couldn't come to parents' day at school or family gatherings. We each got so good at pretending we would sometimes get into arguments over what the real excuse was for her absence. That was good training, because today I am able to deny anything I want. When I beat my wife so bad she needed to be hospitalized, I really believed that she fell and hurt herself. I wasn't lying, I really believed it."

Another side of denial is secrecy. Children learn that no one outside the family is to be trusted with the secret of the parent's addiction. The whole family becomes isolated, but particularly the children, who have nowhere to turn for help. The "parental child" especially has to carry the burden, the secret, the denial, alone.

Some families respond to the out-of-control abuser by becoming over-controlled themselves. No one is allowed to express feelings, everything is done a certain way, with no deviation. One client described dinner time with his alcoholic father:

> "We sat there and no one was allowed to say a word. We had to eat our food in the 'right way' and in the 'right order.' My mother was in charge of keeping us in line for fear that my father would fly off the handle. Sometimes the tension was so great I would walk away from the table with a knot in my stomach."

In chemically dependent families there are usually the "good" and "bad" children. The good children try to do everything right. They try so hard to please at home, in school and in social situations that people don't notice that they are experiencing a great deal of pain and confusion inside. The "bad" kids, on the other hand, get a lot of attention. They get in trouble at school, in social relationships and in the community. Their actions are ways of crying out for help. Sensitive teachers, school counselors and police officers know how to ask about family violence and chemical dependency so as to make the appropriate family interventions.

Two frequent results of growing up in a chemically abusive family are: 1) becoming chemically abusive oneself, and 2) becoming involved with a person who is chemically abusive. But many men who grew up in this type of family never abuse alcohol themselves, or get involved with alcoholics. Just the same, many of these men may still be suffering from the effects of their early experiences. Some men find that they experience addictive patterns just the same as alcoholics, but they are addicted to food, smoking, work, sex, relationships, or love. The man looks to something, or someone, outside himself to relieve the burden, to rescue him from the pain, to give his life some sense of security and meaning.

Men may continue old coping patterns that worked when they were children, but only create new problems as adults. As one client described it,

"When I was a child, my father would get drunk at the dinner table and begin to criticise and put down my siblings, my mother, and me. He would be so cruel sometimes that I would run into my room and hide away for the rest of the evening. Today, every time my wife wants to talk about her feelings about anything, but especially our relationship, I kind of run off to my room. I'm still present physically, but emotionally I have left and I'm in my room, hiding. I am learning to come out a little and listen to what she has to say, but it is really scary sometimes. She'll ask me where I am and I tell her I am up in my room. She knows to back off at that point. She also knows that I will come out some time and be with her."

If any of these ACA patterns apply to you, we suggest that you talk with a counselor experienced in helping adult children of alcoholics. There are groups and classes for you to attend that can help you identify how your childhood experiences affect your life today, and how to change those patterns.

Where To Get Help

A person with an alcohol or drug problem can find help just about anywhere. The Yellow Pages has listings under "Alcoholism Information and Treatment Centers" and "Drug Abuse and Addiction Information and Treatment Centers." "Alcoholics Anonymous" is also listed in the white pages. Programs can be residential, hospital-based, outpatient, self-help or any combination.

Residential programs can be either privately owned or non-profit agencies. A person may stay in the program anywhere from a month to over a year. The advantage of the residential program is that you live with other recovering alcoholics or drug abusers so that you get the continual support you need to stop using. There is always someone there to talk to. Programs vary as to how structured they are and how much counseling you receive. However, the main purpose of the residential program is to help the recovering alcoholic or drug abuser make the necessary changes in his life so that he won't need alcohol or other drugs.

Hospital-based programs are short-term residential programs. The client receives four to twelve weeks of intensive treatment, usually including Alcoholics Anonymous, Narcotics Anonymous, individual and group counseling, family counseling and medication, if needed. This is followed by an after-care program for a period of time. Many hospital and residential programs also have an outpatient service of individual or group counseling. In addition, there are many alcohol and drug programs in the community that offer weekly counseling for you and your family.

Although talking to counselors can be very helpful in addressing this problem, it can be equally helpful to talk with someone who has already been where you have, and can tell you what you can expect in the days ahead. The most well-known self-help programs are Alcoholics Anonymous and Narcotics Anonymous. These programs offer meetings every day, practically throughout the day in larger cities, for persons with alcohol and drug problems. Although going to this meeting may seem difficult, inconvenient and awkward, it is important to develop the necessary support that will help you stop drinking or using. At the same time you will have established contacts, so if you have the urge to go back to your old habits you know where and who you can go to for support. AL-ANON family groups holds meetings like AA, but these meetings are for persons who are family and friends of alcoholics. In addition to AA and AL-ANON there are groups and counselors in your community that specialize in helping adult children of alcoholics or ACA.

Persons who attend AA, ALANON or NA will have what's known as a sponsor help them through the early stages of recovery. A sponsor is a person who is already well into his recovery. Your sponsor is a person to call when you feel the urge to drink, use or act out in other ways. He is someone with whom you can discuss your difficulties and successes during your recovery. He is someone who has experienced many of the same emotions you are feeling inside. He has walked and is still walking the same path as you. Most important, he is someone who has worked and is still working on the steps to recovery.

The Twelve Steps of AA and NA are the key to sobriety. They are rules for healthy and positive living. The Twelve Steps can help any person who is trying to overcome personal difficulties. Some men who have been to AA or NA have stated that they were turned off by the mention of God. It is important to know that AA and NA are not religions, nor do they advocate any one particular religion. However, they do advocate spirituality as an important part of the recovery process. Religion is a particular system of faith and worship that advocates for a particular god or gods, whereas spirituality is a personal quest that doesn't necessarily involve any religion's god. The reason why AA advocates the seeking of a higher power is because alcoholics and drug addicts are notorious for wanting to do things their way. This is called self-willing; "I can do it myself, I don't need any help." The truth is he hasn't done it himself, and he is out of control of his chemical use. He needs to turn to a higher power that will help overcome his urges, some greater force that will remind him of what he needs to do to stay sober.

Aside from spirituality, following the Twelve Steps will improve a person's life in many ways. When men ask "How can I get sober or recover from my violence problems?", the answer is in the word "HOW" — Honesty, Openness and Willingness. You need to be honest with yourself and others. You need to be open to the Twelve Steps and the AA or NA fellowship, and you need to be willing to go to all lengths to get sober and stop your violence. That's **how** AA and NA works.

If chemicals are a problem in your life, it will be necessary to face it if you expect to stop your violent behavior. Get an assessment by a qualified chemical dependency counselor, and get treatment if it's recommended. We have found that men who continue to use mood-altering chemicals will not benefit as much from anger and violence counseling as those who abstain. Therefore, we encourage you to stop all use for a period of time until you have your behavior under control. Perhaps you will discover that you don't need chemicals at all.

Study Questions

1. How have mood-altering chemicals affected your violence?

2. How has your use affected your family members?

3. How does your family member's use of alcohol and/or other drugs affect you?

4. What are your reasons for using chemicals?

5. What would your life be like without alcohol and/or other drugs?

6. How were alcohol and/or other drugs used in your family when you were a child? How did those experiences affect you then? How do they affect you now?

7. In what stage of the chemical use progression are you?

Anger Journal

Date			
Intensity	1 2 3 4 5 6 7 8 9 10		1 2 3 4 5 6 7 8 9 10
Physical Signs			
Behavior Signs			
Situation			
Did you take a Time-Out?	Yes | No Comments		Yes | No Comments
Did you Stuff it, Escalate it, Direct it?	Stuff it | Escalate it Comments | Direct it		Stuff it | Escalate it Comments | Direct it
"I" Statements	I'm feeling		I'm feeling
Physical Activity			
Alcohol or Drug use?	Yes | No Comments		Yes | No Comments

CHAPTER SIX

LEARNING TO LISTEN TO OTHERS

In our years of counseling couples, it never ceases to amaze us how hard it is for two people to really listen to what the other person is saying. It is almost as if two people are speaking different languages. Usually, instead of listening, one person thinks about what he wants to say next while the other person is talking. Listening to others is a skill, and a difficult one to develop.

Listening to someone get angry at us is probably the most difficult experience most of us can imagine — it can really touch some sensitive nerves. Why? Each of us has our own reasons. Some may not even know why, but only that we have a strong reaction to it. Let's talk about some of the more common reasons people react defensively or angrily to someone telling them, "**I feel angry at you!**"

Defensive Reactions to Anger

If a person reacts defensively, it's usually because he feels under attack in some way, and is trying to protect himself. Very often anger feels like a verbal attack. If your partner is angry at you, you may feel she is trying to tell you something about you through her anger — that you are bad or wrong. If you grew up in a family where anger was expressed through put-downs or humiliation you are likely to interpret your partner's anger as a statement about yourself. However, anger, when expressed directly, is simply a person's way of letting you know what they are feeling inside. If you interpret their anger as a statement about yourself you are likely to feel defensive, and unlikely to hear what they are really trying to say in the first place.

Do you hear your partner's anger as a criticism of yourself?

Do you respond to her anger defensively?

Think about the times you have felt anger toward someone. For example, you might feel angry because you didn't like what someone has said or done. It usually feels better just to communicate your anger. But if the listener acts defensive, you are likely to feel as though you weren't heard. One purpose for expressing anger is just to get it off your chest. Another reason is to let the other person know how they or a particular situation **affects** you. But a third and important reason for expressing your anger is to feel more intimate with your partner.

How does expressing anger promote intimacy? When you share your anger with your partner, you are telling her that you trust her to stay with you even though you're expressing these powerful and scary feelings. You are saying, "I want to communicate with you. I want to feel this feeling but also keep contact with you in a way that can heal the anger. I want you to understand that I can be angry, and still in control of myself." In this way communicating anger can actually promote intimacy.

If you have a difficult time hearing your partner's anger, you are also going to have problems helping your partner get beyond her anger. Steve and Linda were in couples counseling for eight months when they finally had a breakthrough. Linda explains:

"For months I've been telling Steve how angry I am at this or that. I tried to tell him when I was feeling angry about the violence. His response most of the time would be to tune me out. When he would respond he would say, 'Do you always have to bring up the past?' or 'Why do you always complain?' Last week I was telling him something about my being angry at how he always forgets to call me when he is inviting friends over dinner and he turned around and said to me, 'I didn't know that makes you angry, I'll try to call next time.' I didn't say anything then, but later that night I was telling him how angry I feel sometimes when I think about the violence. He said to me, 'I know you must feel that way.' You know, I've been feeling a lot less angry this week just because he finally heard me. I don't have to repeat myself so much. He understands!"

For Linda and Steve it was important for each to express the anger directly. But it also made a difference when the listener really heard and understood it. Both expressing and hearing anger in this way will decrease the intensity of anger and the likelihood of violence.

If you always assume that people are criticizing you when they express anger, life will be very difficult. You may begin to feel that you have to change something about yourself every time your partner expresses her anger. At that moment you don't have to change anything, all you **have** to do is listen. Afterwards, you may need some time to think about what the other person said and wants from you. You can weigh it in your mind when you are not in the middle of a barrage of emotion.

Sometimes people respond to anger defensively or angrily because it reminds them of how their parents may have expressed their anger.

In one group a man told how he got extremely agitated when his wife yelled at him. He also told how he became agitated as a child when his father and mother fought or when his father beat him. Those were painful memories. He learned very early that anger was something to be afraid of, because it usually led to violence and hurt feelings. He began to associate anger with violence and pain.

How do you respond when your partner expresses her anger?

How does it remind you of your childhood?

Some men get defensive or angry when their wife or lover gets angry at them, because they view an argument as a win or lose situation. Someone has to be right and someone has to be wrong. It is our experience that both people can be right and both people can be wrong. In fact, it usually doesn't matter. But if it matters to you, then there are going to be times when you feel that your partner is telling you you're wrong or bad. This may cause you to feel attacked and your response may be to defend yourself.

Do you see arguments as right and wrong, win and lose situations?

How does this attitude affect your ability to hear anger?

50

As we discussed earlier, part of the upbringing or training men receive backs them into a corner, leaving little room for them to be fallible, and human. Not only does the man have to do everything the "right way," but he has to make sure those around him do things the same way so that the result will be "right." It is our belief that people argue, not because one is right and the other is wrong, but because people are different. And because people are different, people will have different expectations in a relationship. People will do things differently and even see things differently. Try this experiment. Put a half glass of water on the table in front of you and your partner. What do you see? You may say you see a glass **half full** of water. What does your partner see? She may see a glass **half empty** of water. Who is right? You both are. Each from your own perspective sees it differently from the other person. Different is not necessarily bad. It's just different. Difference is what gives the world color and contrast. Imagine what it would be like living with someone exactly like you, with not only your positive traits, but also all your idiosyncrasies, quirks, and nasty habits. After a while you might begin to welcome some differences.

Another reason men may react defensively to hearing someone express anger or criticism of them, is that they may not like those same things about themselves. And who likes to be reminded of his shortcomings? A man in our group was always late to appointments. Late to group, late to work, late to dates with his girl friend. His friends constantly harassed him about it. And justifiably so — no one likes to be kept waiting. Over time he had grown to dislike this part of himself, but hadn't gotten it together to do something about it. It had also become a sore spot for him; and when his partner got angry at him for being late, he became very defensive.

Often when a partner gets angry at us or expresses dislike of a part of us, it's the part of us that **we** don't like either. Think about this for a few minutes. Can you think of things your partner doesn't like about you, or often gets frequently angry at you about? How do you feel about these things? Are they things about yourself that you'd like to change as well?

Exercise: Likes and Dislikes

Write down three things about yourself that you don't like and have heard other people complain about.

1._____

2._____

3._____

Imagine your partner getting angry at or critical of these parts of you. What would your usual defensive response be? How could you respond non-defensively?

Once a man can honestly identify those parts of himself he wants to change, he has taken the first step to actually changing those characteristics. Changing may be difficult and takes conscious effort. You may want to talk with a counselor about making these changes. But the key is your ability to identify and take responsibility for your own "sore spots," especially when you find yourself getting defensive with your partner.

No matter what your reason for getting defensive, you need to remind yourself that anger is anger — nothing more and nothing less. Like all emotions, it will pass, if **you accept it**. If you fight it, it will bug you forever.

Women and Anger

We have found that when there has been ongoing violence in a relationship, the person being assaulted will feel a great deal of anger and resentment. But she is in a very difficult situation, because if she expresses her anger and resentment, she is likely to get hit again. If she doesn't express it directly, it eventually comes out in indirect ways, such as emotional or sexual withdrawal, sarcasm, teasing, complaining, constantly being annoyed or irritated, or not following through on commitments. These indirect ways of expressing anger are likely to cause a fight anyway. It is easy to see why the result is a woman who becomes depressed and withdrawn, and says "good-bye" to the relationship.

When a man starts counseling, we find that the couple may go through a honeymoon period, when both people feel good, close and happy again. It may even seem as though the violence never happened.

But this period begins to fade, and old patterns begin to emerge. This period is very similar to the "calm, loving, respite" stage of the cycle of violence, described earlier.

After the man has been in counseling for a period of time, and trust begins to be re-established in the relationship, the woman may find that it becomes less and less threatening to assert her feelings, especially her negative feelings. These feelings may be about what the man is saying or doing now; the feelings may also be about what has happened in the past. He's probably thinking, "Why bring up the past? It's over with." He needs to understand that she has probably kept this resentment and anger inside for a long time. She **needs** to express this anger or it will continue to come up in indirect ways.

This anger about the past violence will be the most difficult anger for you to hear. Yet she needs to express it, and you need to hear it. You may get defensive. As we said above, it will remind you of a part of yourself you're not particularly proud of. So your impulse will be to defend yourself, make her stop talking about the past and to view it as her problem. But Stop! Take a deep breath. Look for your anger cues. If you begin to feel angry when she expresses her anger, take a Time-Out.

Exercises: Responding to Others' Anger

There are many reasons why men may react defensively to anger expressed by others. You probably have your own reasons that we haven't discussed. But, if you are in charge of your own reactions, you can begin to have a meaningful exchange with someone. Even if it's anger, it can have a positive outcome.

What can you do in the midst of a barrage of anger from someone else? How can you prevent your response from escalating to violence? Here are a few options:

1. Take a deep breath — and another. Count to five to yourself while inhaling. Count to five to yourself while exhaling. Deep breathing can have a relaxing effect on you.

2. If you begin to feel angry — take a Time-Out. You'll feel less angry just by telling her you are doing so. After your Time-Out, come back and talk about what happens to you when she expresses her anger at you. Remember, use "I" statements.

3. Talk about this chapter with your wife or lover before you get into an argument. Discussing this issue can really clear the air so that when the time comes that she's angry at you, you may feel less need to be angry back or defend yourself.

4. Try the following exercise with your partner or a friend. Each of you sit in a chair facing each other, so that your heads are about an equal height. Have your partner or friend say the following to you: "I'm feeling angry at you!" Have her begin saying it in a soft voice, then continue to repeat the statement until she says it louder and louder, until she is very loud. "I FEEL ANGRY AT YOU!" Discuss with each other what it was like saying it and what it was like hearing it. Then switch roles. You begin softly with "I'm feeling angry at you," then louder and louder until you're very loud. Discuss again what it was like hearing it and what it was like saying it. Sometimes just hearing the words may help you become less sensitive to hearing them when they are really meant.

5. Think about the following: what do you want from your wife or lover when you are feeling angry? Do you want to be held? Do you want to be alone? Do you want her to tell you she understands your anger? Do you want someone to try to talk you out of it? Do you want someone to tell you that you are wrong for feeling that way? Do you want someone just to listen? Think about it and talk to your partner about what it is that **you** want. Find out what **she** wants. If you know ahead of time, it will help you when you're confronted with the situation.

During the next few weeks, try to be aware of your reactions to people, especially your partner, when they are feeling angry with you. Come back and re-read this chapter if you find yourself having trouble listening to anger non-defensively.

Study Questions

1. Discuss with the group your responses to your partner when she expresses her anger.

2. How do you know when your partner is angry?

3. How do you act **defensively** towards your partner's anger?

4. How do you act **non-defensively** towards your partner's anger?

5. Does your partner express her anger about past incidents of violence? How do you make it difficult for her to talk about her feelings?

6. What do you want from your partner when you express your anger? What does she want from you when she expresses her anger?

Anger Journal

Date				
Intensity	1 2 3 4 5 6 7 8 9 10		1 2 3 4 5 6 7 8 9 10	
Physical Signs				
Behavior Signs				
Situation				
Did you take a Time-Out?	Yes	No	Yes	No
	Comments		Comments	
Did you Stuff it, Escalate it, Direct it?	Stuff it	Escalate it	Stuff it	Escalate it
	Comments	Direct it	Comments	Direct it
"I" Statements	I'm feeling		I'm feeling	
Physical Activity				
Alcohol or Drug use?	Yes	No	Yes	No
	Comments		Comments	

CHAPTER SEVEN

FEELINGS AND COMMUNICATION

Earlier, we talked about anger, how to recognize it and how to manage it. Anger is just one of many feelings that we experience every day. We have found that feelings serve a definite purpose, and they are often present even when we least expect them. This chapter will look at the nature of feelings, how we can recognize them, and what usefulness they have in our daily lives.

Ray was sent by the court to our office for counseling. He had grabbed his wife by the hair and thrown her to the kitchen floor during an argument at dinner. This was the third violent incident in several months, and his wife called the police, who arrested Ray and took him briefly to the county jail. Instead of a jail term or a fine, Ray was given the choice of counseling. As we talked to him, Ray complained about the unfairness of the criminal proceedings against him. "Beth hit me with a serving spoon two weeks ago and I didn't call the cops on her. She taunted me that night and knew what I'd do." When we asked him his feelings about being arrested, he said, "I told you. I feel it's unfair; she shouldn't have done it." As we continued to talk it became clear that we were using the word "feelings" in a quite different way from Ray. As we discuss this difference you will see why many men have difficulty in talking about their feelings.

What are feelings? Feelings are an inner emotional response to our experience that tell us about the **value** of that experience to us. There are many words that are used to describe feelings: elated, sad, frustrated, frightened, happy, angry, depressed — all describe inner emotional responses. Some words describe degrees of feelings; for example, "irritated" may mean just a little angry, and "outraged," a lot. Some words combine different feelings; "upset" may often mean angry and hurt, for example. This was part of the problem for Ray. When we talked to him it turned out that he had a mixture of feelings and didn't really know how to sort them out. He was very angry at Beth — he hadn't realized just **how** angry. He was also frightened about the consequences of being arrested; yet a part of him felt relieved that something was being done to bring his violence under control before it got worse.

When we have an emotional response to something, we are evaluating its meaning to us. Most men are trained from an early age to make these evaluations by using only rational means — by thinking. We see something happening and add up the pluses and minuses. Then we have a judgment of what that thing means. Often we do not pay attention to our feeling response. Thinking and feeling are two different ways of doing the same thing. Ray was using his thinking response to make a judgment about his situation; he added up the facts and decided "it was unfair." But he said he **felt** it was unfair. Does that make sense to you? Unfair is not a feeling. As we understand it, Ray's feelings were stirred up, but he didn't know how to describe them exactly. He wound up expressing his **feelings** in terms of his **thinking**.

One thing we see men commonly do is to confuse feelings with thinking or observation. For example:

"I feel it was unfair."

"I feel that you are going to leave me."

"I feel you are trying to get me angry."

These statements are "I feel-thinking" statements rather than "I feel-emotion" statements. A good test for whether a statement is an "I feel-thinking" statement, is to replace "I feel" with "I think." If it makes sense, then it is probably more of a thinking statement or observation rather than a feeling statement. How can we change the above "I feel-thinking" statements to "I feel-emotion" statements?

"I feel your calling the police was unfair."

"I feel **hurt** that you called the police on me."

"I feel that you are going to leave me."

"I feel **sad** that you are going to leave me."

"I feel you are trying to get me angry."

"I **do not like** what you are saying to me."

The purpose of expressing feelings is to communicate to other people how we experience the world. That is, how we are **affected** by what they do or say.

As we talked further, Ray realized that his feelings told him he had been hurt and his thinking told him that he didn't deserve that hurt. It actually felt **better** to him to say "I feel hurt" than "I feel it was unfair."

Following is a list of words. We would like you to say each of them out loud, perhaps two or three times. Try out different tones of voice for each word, or say it louder or softer. Pay attention to your physical feelings as you say each word. Write in other words you use to describe your feelings. What memories does each stir up in you? When you are finished, underline the three words you respond to most strongly.

List of Feelings

excited	frustrated	hurt	_____
tender	frightened	jealous	_____
sad	contented	loving	_____
lonely	depressed	elated	_____
edgy	timid	happy	_____

If you are like most men in our society, you are not likely to be aware of your feelings all that often. A number of factors get in the way. First, as men we are taught that feelings are either not that important, or they are downright dangerous. We are taught that feelings are unpredictable, explosive, unmanly, irrational and unfair. If a man exhibits angry feelings, including violence, he may be seen as powerful but untrustworthy. If he shows soft feelings he will probably be seen as weak and "womanish." It is very difficult for a man to change this image in our society, even though all men have feelings, and also have the urge to express them.

Also, when we are not aware of our feelings we can avoid facing the consequences of those feelings. It was convenient for Ray to be unaware of his anger at Beth, for example. Once aware of it, he had to make some choice about what to do with it, from stuffing it to escalating to directing it. None of his choices were very easy for him. If he was aware of his fear, he had to identify himself as frightened, which is not a pleasant way for most of us to see ourselves. All in all, it is easier to pretend the feelings are not there, or just be unaware of them.

We may also suppress our feelings because we don't want to deal with another person's response to them. Even though Ray felt better saying "I felt hurt" in our office, he very much doubted that he could say the same thing to Beth. He worried that she would see him as weak and wouldn't respect him. He was also afraid that he would be too vulnerable to her, and she would use the opportunity to hurt him even more. These concerns are often quite real; but after you are aware of your feelings, it is your choice whether, and how, to express them. You may choose **not** to express your feelings in situations that leave you vulnerable to hurt. They are **your** feelings, and you are in control of their expression.

Feelings may also be very frightening and confusing. Mark witnessed his father severely beat his mother throughout his childhood. At the time he felt helpless to do anything about it. He hated his father for his violence, and felt a great deal of pain inside for many years. He became a successful businessman in a field that discouraged any expression of emotion. He spent his life avoiding any situation where he might feel the anger and the pain. When those feelings did occasionally surface, he would feel overwhelmed and unable to manage them. In his third marriage, he became physically and psychologically abusive. In counseling he began to talk about his childhood experiences, and for the first time in his adult life he expressed his anger toward his father and mother. His anger eventually turned into tears, and those deep wounds began to heal.

Given all these obstacles and problems, why **should** you want to be more aware of your feelings? We've already mentioned part of the answer to this. Feelings give you valuable information about yourself and your judgment of whatever situations you are in. We have found that when people make decisions based on both thinking and feeling responses, they are much more likely to be happy with the result.

Another reason to be aware of feelings is to reduce stress. Just in themselves, strong feelings can cause stress, but that stress is often reduced by acknowledging and expressing those feelings. If you have separated from your wife, it is stressful to deal with the sadness you may feel. If you put on a happy face so that no one — maybe not even you — can see that sadness, the stress will build up. Expressing that sadness can get it off your chest and allow you to move on to the next step in your life. As with Mark, expressing feelings can also help to heal old wounds that continue to plague us in relationships, in work and with family.

Awareness of feelings is also a matter of self-protection. How does this work? Men often tell us that they feel manipulated by their wives or partners. In our society women generally tend to be more aware of feelings and express them more readily than men. In a fight, a man may be using his "language" of logic and reason, and a woman may use a different "language" of feeling and emotion. The woman's feeling statements can have a direct effect on the man's feelings even though he's not aware of it. He feels his emotions "jerked around," doesn't know what's happening, and decides he's being manipulated. His frustration in this may contribute to a violent outburst. If a man can be aware of his feelings, he will be more likely to see what is going on; he can express his own feelings in return, and he'll feel less frustrated and manipulated.

There is another important reason to be aware of feelings. By expressing our feelings directly, we can be truly effective and in control of ourselves in relationships. This is where communication comes in, and we will talk about this whole issue a little later.

How can you be more aware of your feelings and express them more clearly? You've already taken the first step by saying those feeling words earlier this chapter. As you said them, you may have noticed that not all the responses inside you were thoughts or ideas. Feelings give us physical sensations as well. In Chapter 4 we talked about the physical signs of anger, and you may be pretty good at recognizing them by now. Sadness, fear, happiness, and hurt, all have their own physical signs as well.

Physical Response to Feelings

Turn back a few pages and look at your list of feelings. As you say the words this time, pay special attention to your physical response to each word. Write down in the space below your physical responses to three of the words on the list. You can use this awareness as a key to recognizing other feelings, just as you did for anger.

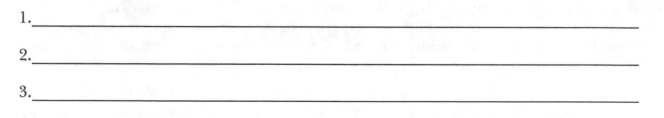

1._____

2._____

3._____

Exercise: Feeling Identification

Another exercise to sharpen your awareness of feelings is to list particular situations in the past when you **have** been aware of feelings. Take your time. Really think about each incident you list. Try also to remember what physical responses you may have experienced in each situation.

Identify three situations in the past month when you felt **happy.**

1._____

2._____

3._____

Identify three situations in the past month when you felt **sad.**

1._____

2._____

3._____

Identify three situations in the past month when you felt **afraid.**

1._____

2._____

3._____

Identify three characteristics about your wife, lover or a close friend that you **like.**

1._____

2._____

3._____

Identify three characteristics about your wife, lover or a close friend that you **do not like.**

1._____

2._____

3._____

Identify three characteristics about your wife, lover or a close friend that **remind you of yourself.**

1._____

2._____

3._____

How do you feel about the things that remind you of yourself? Do you **like** or **dislike** them? Is it OK to like or not like things about yourself? Sometimes the things we **like least** about another person are the same things we do not like about ourselves.

Let Others Know Your Feelings

The next step after being aware of feelings is expressing them. As we discussed before, feelings have a natural function in helping us know how we react to our experiences. They also have a natural function in communicating to others who we are. In fact, we almost always communicate our feelings in some way to those we are close to. If we don't do it with words, we usually do it by body posture, tone of voice, silence, or facial expression. Often we try to cover up our feelings, and what we say is very different from what we feel. This may lead to confusion, since we may express one thing in words and another — maybe even opposite — thing in our tone of voice or gestures. That confusion may be a smokescreen that keeps you safe, but when there is confusion in a relationship there is not much trust, and the relationship inevitably goes downhill. So, being effective in an intimate relationship, being who you are and building a solid trusting relationship, all depend on expressing your feelings directly.

How do you do this? Each person has his own way of expressing feelings. Earlier in this book we talked about ways of expressing anger directly. How would you express sadness to your partner? Some men might cry, though that is not often easy to do. You might simply say, "I feel sad." You might ask your partner to hold you. If you think about it, you could probably come up with your own ways of showing sadness.

Exercise: Feeling Communication

Now try this exercise. Imagine a situation where you felt sad (perhaps one that you listed earlier). Write down three ways you could have expressed that feeling directly in the situation. Use your imagination and write down whatever ways you can think of — even if you might not be able to actually do them.

1._____

2._____

3._____

60

Many men tell us that they aren't aware of their feelings until some time after they occur. Remember that it is okay to "fill in the blanks" later if you don't recognize a feeling when it happens. If you feel sad or angry that your wife went to the movies while you had to work at night, you can tell her the next day. It will still work!

What do you do if you are having difficulty identifying your feelings? The best way to start is by identifying your physical sensations. As with anger, your body may be feeling a feeling long before your mind has interpreted that sensation. One night in our group Lee was having difficulty talking about his feelings. He was describing how his mother and father placed him up for adoption when he was six years old. When one of the other men in the group asked him how he was feeling he responded, "I don't know." He really **didn't** know how he was feeling! One of the group leaders asked him to focus on his body.

Group leader: What sensations do you feel in your body, Lee?

Lee: I have a heavy feeling in my stomach.

Group leader: If that sensation had a voice, what would it say?

Lee: I'm sinking. I am down.

Group leader: Lee, try saying out loud, I am feeling sad, I am feeling rejected.

Lee: I am feeling sad, I am feeling rejected.

Group Leader: Do either one of those statements fit the physical sensation?

Lee: Yes, they both do!

Group leader: Try saying them again and see what happens.

Lee: I am feeling sad. I am feeling rejected.

With that Lee began to leak tears, and even a few sobs came out. Afterwards he felt scared by the intensity of his feelings but at the same time felt a relief. Lee was beginning to learn the language of his feelings.

One final word about expressing feelings. Feelings are a tool for understanding and communication. You **have** the right to say how you feel. You do **not have** the right to expect people to change because of your feelings. That is the risky part. Your partner may hear you express your hurt directly, and she may choose to go on doing what hurts you. You can't make that choice for her, and you can't really even manipulate her into making the choice you want. If she changes her behavior, it will be because she sees clearly who you are and how you feel, and not because she's being forced to change. When you get down to the bottom line, you need to trust your partner's good will toward you; and that is often a very hard step to take. If trust is poor it can be built up through expressing at least some feelings directly, and through expressing your needs clearly, as we discuss next in Chapter 8.

Study Questions

1. Which feelings are you **most** comfortable expressing to your partner?

2. Which feelings are you **least** comfortable expressing to your partner?

3. Which feelings are you most and least comfortable expressing to other men?

4. What makes it hard for you to identify and express those uncomfortable feelings?

5. Describe a situation when you communicated your feelings in a direct, non-intimidating manner to your partner.

6. What do you like about **not** showing your feelings? What is the advantage?

7. If you are having difficulty identifying your feelings, begin with your physical sensations. Then ask yourself, "If that physical sensation had a voice, what would it say?"

Anger Journal

Date					
Intensity	1 2 3 4 5 6 7 8 9 10			1 2 3 4 5 6 7 8 9 10	
Physical Signs					
Behavior Signs					
Situation					
Did you take a Time-Out?	Yes	No		Yes	No
	Comments			Comments	
Did you Stuff it, Escalate it, Direct it?	Stuff it	Escalate it		Stuff it	Escalate it
	Comments	Direct it		Comments	Direct it
"I" Statements	I'm feeling			I'm feeling	
Physical Activity					
Alcohol or Drug use?	Yes	No		Yes	No
	Comments			Comments	

63

CHAPTER EIGHT

BECOMING AN ASSERTIVE MAN!

Perhaps two of the hardest things to do in an intimate relationship are to ask directly for what you want, and to refuse requests. Many of the men we see don't know how to ask for what they want, so instead they demand and order. It is a big risk to ask directly and clearly for what you want in a relationship, because you take the chance of getting your request refused — and that may hurt. But if you ask directly, at least your partner will know what you want. One purpose of this chapter is to give you practice in finding successful ways to ask for what you want, ways that will increase trust and communication with your partner.

On the other hand, others will inevitably make requests of you. If you don't like a request, you can either go along with whatever is asked of you and secretly become resentful, or you can learn to say "no." Many of the men in our program stuff it when they want to say "no"; and of course, eventually the pressure cooker builds up and there is an explosion. This chapter will also begin to give you practice at being aware of when you want to say "no," and then saying it!

Let's listen in on a group discussion focusing on asking for your needs, and saying "no."

Richard: When I got married, I kind of figured my wife would be like my mother. She always knew what my father wanted — or at least it seemed that way. But after our honeymoon it was a really different story. We were always getting our lines of communication crossed. I came home late, and the dinner was sitting on the table cold. I came home on time the next night, and there was no dinner. She couldn't keep track of my schedule. She used to say, "What schedule? I don't know your schedule. You never tell me when you're going to be home." It took me a couple of years to get it through my head that she really couldn't read my mind. I remember one Monday night I came home and I was watching the football game. I was sitting there getting mad for an hour before she offered me a beer. I thought she should have known I would want a beer while watching the game.

Don: I consider myself an easygoing guy. I am usually willing to bend over backwards for a friend. I know I tend to get walked over, so when that happens I just stop seeing that friend. Whenever my wife asks me something, I say "yes." Now I am learning that sometimes I say "yes" when I really mean "no." The other day I was working on my car. It was the only day that week that I could get the plugs and oil changed. My wife asked me if I would go shopping with her. I said "yes." We went to one store after another. I didn't realize it was going to take all day. On the way back I remembered we had tickets to a concert that night. My car wasn't going to get done. I began to burn. She said something, I really don't even remember what it was. I'm sure it wasn't a big deal, but I blew up at her. I told her what she was doing wrong, and how she can't do anything right. Later that night I realized I could have avoided that whole thing if I had asserted myself in the first place. But I didn't want to let her down. Especially after all the violence. I wanted to be nice to her. But then, that's part of the reason I was violent in the first place. I want to be nice and then I forget about my needs. My father was like that, too.

Sonny: My dad used to order everyone around. He was this drill sergeant, literally. He came home from work and we had to line up by the front door. Then he gave us the orders for the night. As much as I hated it then, I started doing that with my wife. I'd find myself ordering her rather than asking. And if I did ask, it was really an order because there was no room for her to disobey. If she did, I got real angry and sometimes hit her. It's been real hard asking instead of ordering her, and knowing she **can** say "no." I could never say "no" as a kid. She told me that she would not stay if I kept ordering her around. I had to look at that one pretty closely. It meant being with my family or being alone.

William: I realized recently that I haven't been able to ask for help at work because I'm afraid of them thinking that I am stupid or incompetent. I'm also afraid that I wouldn't get the help that I need even if I did ask. After realizing this, my counselor asked me if I could ask my wife for help. I couldn't think of one time in twenty years of marriage that I ever asked her for help. I assume that I should know how to do everything. If I didn't know how to do something I just wouldn't do it or I'd fake it. So the other day I was starting the barbecue and I went into the kitchen where Leslie was preparing a sauce for the meat. I tasted the sauce and it was great. I turned to Leslie and said, "How do you make that?" She told me this and that, she was very vague. She went on to tell me that I don't need to bother myself with those details. Then I asked her, could she show me how to make that sauce so I can do it next time? I really don't know how to cook sauces. She was pretty uncomfortable, so I told her about my session with my counselor. She was really touched by my asking her for help. She hugged me and told me that she loved me. Talk about surprise. All that just by asking for help.

These men all have different reasons why it's difficult for them to ask for what they want. Although rationally, we don't expect our partners to read our minds, we sometimes act as if that is what we do expect. Why does this happen? Many men never learned in their own families how to communicate their needs and feelings in a positive and non-intimidating way. Like violence, non-assertiveness is learned. Another reason some men are afraid of asserting their needs is because of an expectation that they won't get what they want; they will be rejected. This fear may be based on low self-esteem. Do I deserve to get what I want —to be heard and understood? Some men don't ask for what they want because they haven't really thought about their needs. Usually they are so involved with sensing or figuring out others' needs that they haven't stopped to pay attention to what their own needs are.

Exercise: Asking for What You Want

What are some of the reasons it is difficult for you to ask for what you want?

1._____

2._____

3._____

When was the last time you **directly** said **no** to someone? If you're like most people, it's probably difficult for you to even remember. Learning to say "no" is as important as learning to ask for what you want. When a man has grown up in a family where the father was a dictator, or passive or absent, he hasn't had an assertive male role model from which to learn these skills. Many men are afraid that they will hurt their partner's feelings if they say "no." Others are afraid the other person will get angry as a result of their saying "no." Some men believe that you do what people want you to do, it is just the right thing to do. You may also have trouble saying "no" to someone when you don't know what you want or how you feel. One man in our group would frequently agree to one thing or another, and then break his commitment. When someone asked him a favor, he would automatically say "yes" but not really think about what was being asked of him. Later, he would think about it and change his mind. Of course, he wouldn't tell the other person, because he wanted to be a "nice guy." So he conveniently forgot his agreement. Finally, he learned how to make an important statement that solved many of his problems: "I need to think about that for a while, I'll get back to you later."

This non-assertive pattern can be just as true for your partner as for you. If you find that you frequently ask her for something that she agrees to, but then doesn't follow through on, you have some choices about how to respond. It is important for you to understand that many battered women are hesitant of asserting themselves for fear of their partner's anger and violence. If you can remember this fact at the time this occurs, you are more likely to respond in a constructive manner. You can stop, take a deep breath, and directly ask if she is feeling afraid of saying "no" with you. If she says, "yes," give her some time to talk about her feelings. If she says "no," perhaps you can discuss this chapter with her.

Most of us refuse requests, but do so in indirect ways. For example, when was the last time someone wanted you to go out with them, but you wanted to stay at home alone? If you're like most people you would have either said "Yes, I'll go along with you," or "I have a business meeting," or "I have a date with my lady." It's difficult for most people to just say, "No, I don't want to go out tonight." Or how about the last time you were at a friend's house for a dinner party. You're getting bored or you just want to leave. As you start to leave, your host says, "Just stay a little while, won't you?" What do you usually say? "No, I would really like to leave," or how about old faithful, "I have to get up early tomorrow," or "I'm not feeling well." For many of us, the word "no" is not even a part of our every day vocabulary. It is not only important to learn **to** say "no," but also **how** to say "no" as well.

Exercise: Saying "No"

What are some of the reasons its difficult for you to say "no?"

1._____

2._____

3._____

Just because you do things according to a pattern doesn't mean you're stuck with it for life. The trick is to get **practice** at changing that pattern.

Learning to Assert Yourself

What are the advantages of asking for what you want? Surprisingly to many people, the first advantage is to **increase** the chance of getting what you want in life. Though there is no guarantee you will always get your way, the odds are more in your favor than if you do not ask, and expect others to read your mind. Just as with yourself, the person you are asking has the right to say "yes" or "no," with or without an explanation. With this in mind, let's begin with some practice in asking for what you want.

Exercise: Assertiveness

Get two chairs facing each other. You sit in one and imagine your wife or girl friend in the other. Make the following requests out loud and see how it feels to ask. Are there any areas that feel more or less comfortable? Rate the difficulty of each request on a 1 to 5 scale (1 being easy and 5 being difficult). Write down any requests not listed that would be especially hard for you. Explain why some were more difficult.

___ 1. I would like to borrow five dollars from you.

___ 2. Would you be willing to help me clean the garage today?

___ 3. I would like to be alone today.

___ 4. I would like to have sex with you.

___ 5. I would like to borrow one hundred dollars.

___ 6. Will you hold me? Im feeling scared.

___ 7. Will you sleep close to me tonight?

___ 8. I would like to sleep alone tonight.

___ 9. I would like a date with you on Friday.

___ 10. I would like to talk quietly.

___ 11. Will you kiss me?

___ 12. I would like to know why you are angry with me.

___ 13. Will you take care of the kids today?

___ 14. How are you feeling today?

___ 15. I would like to read the paper; can we talk later?

___ 16. I would like to take a Time-Out.

___ 17. _____

___ 18. _____

___ 19. _____

Repeat the exercise, but this time imagine that your partner is making the requests. Say "no" to each one. Pay attention to which ones are harder than others to refuse. Rate the difficulty of each request on a 1 to 5 scale (1 being easy and 5 being difficult). Explain why some were more difficult.

Exercise: Who Can You Assert Yourself With?

Think about who you can directly ask for what you want and who you can say "no" to. Note whether this would be Difficult, Easy, or Somewhat Uncomfortable.

Example: Mother: **Somewhat Uncomfortable**

Father	Mother	Wife	Attorney
Boss	Minister	Male friend	Female friend
Son	Daughter	Grandson	Granddaughter
Police officer	Counselor	Doctor	Store salesperson
Phone survey	Work colleague	Neighbor	Mother-in-law
Father-in-law	Sister-in-law	Brother	Sister
Door-door salesperson	Work supervisor	Your employee	Rabbi

I Can't vs. I Won't

Which of these expressions do you use when you want to say "no?" Often people will say "I can't" when they really mean "I won't." There is a difference between the two expressions. When you say "I won't," you are indicating that you are making a choice; that you are choosing to say "no" rather than agree. When you say "I can't," you are suggesting that there is some force beyond your control, that is preventing you from doing something. And if you say "I can't" enough, you may even make yourself **feel** out of control. In some cases, you may actually not be able to make a choice; for example, going running with a leg in a cast, or on a date when you really do have other plans. But many times, we do use "I can't" when we really mean "I won't," or "I don't want to." Try to be aware of the words you typically use when you're refusing requests.

Why?

Some of the time when you say "no" you're likely to get a "why" in return. And persistent "whys" can ultimately lead to an escalation and possibly violence. One of the nice things about saying "no" is that you don't **owe** anybody an explanation, if you don't want to give one. On the other hand, you may **want** to explain; what you do is your choice. For example:

Mary: John, will you go with me to a movie?

John: No, I don't want to.

Mary: Why not?

John: I just don't want to.
   or
   I'm resting now so I don't want to get up and go to a movie.
   or
   I just want to sit around the house and watch TV tonight — but can we go another time?

If you give a reason, it doesn't matter whether that reason is "good enough"; what's important is that it's **your** reason. The other person may persist in asking why, whether you explain or not. If this happens, and you find yourself getting angry, take a Time-Out!

Learning to say "no" and handling the consequences takes a lot of practice. This may be an issue you would like to focus on in counseling; if so, bring it up with your counselor and spend some time working on saying "no."

Assertiveness, Non-assertiveness and Aggressiveness

Assertive behavior is what we have been discussing throughout this chapter and in other parts of this workbook. It is an attempt to communicate clearly and directly your needs, thoughts and feelings. Non-assertive behavior is the opposite. It is **not** directly communicating your needs, thoughts or feelings. People fail to assert themselves for a variety of reasons, some of which were discussed earlier in this chapter.

Aggressiveness is another way to make your needs known. Aggressiveness is **not** caring about other people's rights. It can be dominating, defensive, hostile and even humiliating. It may be expressing your needs, thoughts and feelings, but it is always at the expense of others.

We believe that both aggressive and non-assertive behavior contribute to violence in relationships. As a matter of fact, this discussion may sound very familiar to you. Try these equations: non-assertiveness = stuffing; aggressiveness = escalating; assertiveness = directing. Two of these three can easily lead to violence. But whether or not violence occurs, unassertive (stuffing) and aggressive (escalating) behavior have an effect on you. You usually will end up feeling guilty, with lower self-esteem, less self-confidence, and less security in your relationship. On the other hand, people who assert themselves (directing), more often feel good about themselves and their relationships.

Like recognizing your anger and taking Time-Outs, assertiveness takes time to learn. Don't expect drastic changes overnight. But **do** expect changes in time. How much time? That depends on you. But what we can say is that the more you practice, the quicker the changes will come.

Assertiveness Homework

You can begin to learn how to assert yourself by practice, and as in building any skill, it's best to start with easier steps. Look down your list on page 68 and choose the persons that you marked as Easy or Somewhat Uncomfortable. If you ranked everyone as Difficult, try to choose those persons you feel may be less difficult than others. Make direct requests of these people this week. Be sure to use an "I" statement followed by a clear request. Write down the request — how it felt and how you could improve the way in which you expressed it. Were there any ways in which you were indirect (escalating or stuffing)? Also note when you refuse requests this week. Remember, clearly saying "no" when appropriate will help others take your requests more seriously.

Study Questions

1. What are your reasons for not asserting yourself?

2. Describe a situation where you might have asserted yourself, but didn't.

3. Describe a situation where you did assert yourself.

4. Practice asking for what you want by going up to your partner or a friend and making a request.

5. Practice saying "no" by going to your partner or a friend and saying "no" to a request that she or he makes of you.

6. Define assertiveness, aggressiveness and non-assertiveness.

Anger Journal

Date		
Intensity	1 2 3 4 5 6 7 8 9 10	1 2 3 4 5 6 7 8 9 10
Physical Signs		
Behavior Signs		
Situation		
Did you take a Time-Out?	Yes No Comments	Yes No Comments
Did you Stuff it, Escalate it, Direct it?	Stuff it Escalate it Comments Direct it	Stuff it Escalate it Comments Direct it
"I" Statements	I'm feeling	I'm feeling
Physical Activity		
Alcohol or Drug use?	Yes No Comments	Yes No Comments

71

CHAPTER NINE

STRESS REDUCTION

We often find that men who batter their partners experience a significant amount of stress, both within their relationships, and in their lives in general. This chapter will discuss what stresses are and where they come from, how to recognize them, and some strategies to manage them.

What is stress? All of us feel it at times. For some of us stress is a part of our everyday lives. We can sometimes cope with it, but sometimes we can't even get a handle on where the stress comes from. And if we don't understand the stress pattern, it can overpower us with confusion. So, let's start off with a definition:

Stress: a physical and emotional response within us to something we see as a threat. There are two types of stress; stress caused by events, and chronic stress.

Stressful Events

What events in your world cause you stress? For most people there are two main types of stressful events, **loss and change**. The death of a loved one, divorce or separation, being fired from a job — are all severe losses and likely to bring on stress. They are also associated with change. When we face change we rehearse it in our heads; perhaps we worry and imagine ahead of time what the results will be. If these imagined results are negative, or if we feel we won't be able to handle the new situation, we may feel stress. This explains why even positive, good events may sometimes produce severe stress. Below is a list of common stresses. Check off which ones apply to your situation and add any others that you experience.

- Troubles with boss

- Troubles with other people at work

- Promotion at work

- Laid off or fired from work

- Death of someone in the family

- Pregnancy or the birth of a child

- Getting married

- Separation or divorce

- Big increase in number of arguments with partner/wife

- Sexual difficulties

- Family reunion

- In-law troubles

- Serious illness or injury

- Serious problem with health or behavior of family member

- Financial problems

- Arrest or conviction for something serious

- Moving to a different neighborhood or town

Another characteristic of events that cause stress is that we often feel helpless to do anything about them. If something threatens or hurts us and we can't do anything about it, the level of stress will increase. How many of the events you've checked above fit into this category? Are there any other irritating patterns or forces in your life that you feel powerless to change? If you feel that others often make fun of you or ignore you, or don't take you seriously, these can cause stressful patterns. These patterns may be setting up a conflict within you that leads to more stress.

For example, imagine that your boss humiliates you in front of your co-workers. Many factors go to work at once to produce stress: 1) loss — you lose face; 2) change — how will you rebuild your status at work; 3) frustration — because it's unfair and you can't tell your boss off; and 4) conflict — the part of you that wants to tell him off fights with the part that wants to be even more of a good guy so he'll see that you're OK. Can you pick a similar example from your own life, and see how many different ways it produces stress in you?

Chronic Stress

What we've been talking about so far is stress caused by specific events which resolve themselves within a relatively short time. Chronic stress is composed of all the elements we have already mentioned, plus three other factors. First, chronic stress is present, to some degree, every day for weeks, months, or even years. Second, there's no focal point, no way that you can say, "Well, if I only change **this**, the stress will go away." This makes it confusing and irrational. Third, it becomes a habit. We respond to events as if they were stressful, even though they may be perfectly ordinary.

Think back to our definition of stress: stress is a physical and emotional response **within us** to something **we see** as a threat. If you have to make a choice about which restaurant to have dinner at with your wife, do you feel stress? Probably most men would not, but a man dealing with chronic stress might begin worrying early in the day about what could go wrong. By dinner time, making the choice of restaurants could be so stressful that he sabotages the whole evening and ends up with a TV dinner. When we are experiencing chronic stress, we **expect** more stress, and usually manage to get it.

The early signs of stress are often not easy to recognize, but in the long run they can be quite severe. Depression, headache, back pain, high blood pressure, and ulcer disease are often associated with chronic stress. Many women who live with men who batter them also experience this form of chronic stress, and they develop physical reactions to the stress of living in a violent environment. Many people feel that heart disease and cancer may be brought on by stress.

Identifying and Coping With Stress

What can you do to recognize stress before it gets to the point of physical illness? Our bodies provide a kind of early warning system, if we can pay attention to it. The following two exercises will help you learn to identify your stress signals and to counteract the effects of stress on your mind and body.

Exercise: Stress Identification

Take a few minutes and do the following. Sit quietly in an area where you will not be distracted. Notice your breathing pattern: is your breathing fast or slow, in your upper or lower chest, smooth or jerky? Don't try to change the pattern, just observe it. Likewise, pay attention to each of the muscles of your body, beginning at the top of your head and working downwards. Notice how much tension or tightness there is in your scalp muscles, brow, facial muscles, jaw, neck, shoulders, arms and chest, and so on. Again, don't try to change any patterns of tension, just note them carefully and move on.

Now go back to where you checked off or wrote down sources of stress. Pick one of them and hold it in your mind for a few moments; perhaps you could imagine re-living it. Now repeat the exercise above. Pay attention to breathing, and to all of your body's muscles. Are there any differences that you notice?

Almost everyone has difficulty with this exercise at first. You may have trouble even **feeling** your muscles, or the sensations may seem trivial or unimportant. People who have followed through with this exercise, perhaps trying it several times, seem to notice that the sensations in breathing and muscles have specific meaning. They may become aware of stress patterns or particular stresses which are expressed through bodily tension.

When under stress, other small signs may appear. We may be easily confused or not think clearly; we may have an acid stomach, leg pain, head or neck pain; we may start to feel a bit pessimistic about life in general. If you look for your own signs and for the subtle tensions you can recognize in your breathing and muscles, you can more clearly recognize your own responses to stress. Take time to focus on these specific effects of stress on your body. Once you are aware of the stress, there are a number of ways you can begin to reduce it.

The first and most immediate way to reduce stress is called **quieting**. Recently there have been many studies demonstrating the beneficial effects of various forms of meditation and biofeedback exercises. Many of these effects occur because meditation is an effective way of quieting ourselves inside and therefore reducing stress. There are quite a variety of meditation techniques that will work, and you may be interested to try out some that are available in your area.

Exercise: Visual Imagery

There are other ways of quieting that you can practice yourself, however, and two of them are described here. First is visual imagery. Lie down or sit comfortably and pay attention to your breathing as you did in the body awareness exercises. After a few minutes, imagine yourself in a place where you would feel very comfortable; at the beach or out in the woods, or in a special room, for example. In your imagination, use all your senses to experience this comfortable place. If you were at the beach you might see the line of the water with the waves breaking, hear the sound of the waves and nearby birds, feel the warm sun and the sand beneath your body. In your mind's eye you may wish to explore around you, or just relax comfortably in one place. Take as much time as you wish with this exercise — there is no hurry. When you are ready, slowly return to your present surroundings and again observe your breathing for a few moments.

A second method of quieting is the following relaxation exercise.

Exercise: Relaxation

Have a friend read the following relaxation exercise to you. Or, tape it and play it back for yourself. After some practice, you should be able to do it on your own.

Put on some loose clothing and take off your shoes. Find a quiet place with soft lighting where you will not be interrupted. Lie down on your back on a rug, a mat or a firm bed with your legs comfortably spread apart, not together or crossed. Get comfortable.

Now close your eyes...Be aware of your breathing...Take full, deep breaths from your stomach...Inhale through your nose...Exhale through your mouth...Inhale slowly...Exhale slowly...Inhale...Exhale...

Imagine that your thoughts are written on the walls all around you. See yourself walking to the light switch and turning out the lights...It is now completely dark in the room...You can not see anything...You back up to the middle of the room and lay down on a soft mattress...It is completely dark in the room...completely dark.

Take full, deep breaths from your stomach...Inhale through your nose...Exhale through your mouth...Inhale...Exhale...

Tense all the muscles in your body...face...chest...arms...stomach...thighs... calves...feet...toes...Feel the tension...your limbs are tensed...Now exhale — let go of all the tension and RELAX...

Breath slowly...Inhale through your nose...Exhale through your mouth...Inhale... Exhale.

Tense all the muscles in your body...hold it...hold it...hold it...and RELAX...

Keep breathing slowly...from the stomach...Inhale through the nose...Exhale through the mouth...Inhale...Exhale...

Keeping the rest of your body relaxed, tense the muscles in your right leg and foot...Keep them tensed...Everything else relaxed...

Keep breathing...Inhale...Exhale...And release...Do it again...Keep everything else relaxed...Keep breathing...And relax...

Keeping the rest of your body relaxed, tense the muscles in your left leg and foot...Keep them tensed...Everything else relaxed...Keep breathing...Inhale...Exhale...And release...Do it again...Keep everything else relaxed...Keep breathing...And relax...

Keeping the rest of your body relaxed, tense the muscles in your stomach and genitals...Keep them tensed...Everything else relaxed...

Keep breathing...Inhale...Exhale...And release...Do it again...Keep everything else relaxed...Keep breathing...And relax...

Keeping the rest of your body relaxed, tense the muscles in your buttocks and lower back...Keep them tensed...Everything else relaxed...Keep breathing...Inhale...Exhale...And release...Do it again...Keep everything else relaxed...Keep breathing...And relax...

Keeping the rest of your body relaxed, tense the muscles in your shoulders...Keep them tensed...Everything else relaxed...Keep breathing...Inhale...Exhale...And release...Do it again...Keep everything else relaxed...Keep breathing...And relax...

Keeping the rest of your body relaxed, tense the muscles in your right arm and hand...Keep them tensed...Everything else relaxed...

Keep breathing...Inhale...Exhale...And release...Do it again...Keep everything else relaxed...Keep breathing...And relax...

Keeping the rest of your body relaxed, tense the muscles in your left arm and hand...Keep them tensed...Everything else relaxed...Keep breathing...Inhale...Exhale...And release...Do it again...Keep everything else relaxed...Keep breathing...And relax...

Keeping the rest of your body relaxed, tense the muscles in your neck...Keep them tensed...Everything else relaxed...Keep breathing...

Inhale...Exhale...And release...Do it again...Keep everything else relaxed...Keep breathing...And relax...

Keeping the rest of your body relaxed, tense the muscles in your face and jaw...Keep them tensed...Everything else relaxed...Keep breathing...Inhale...Exhale...And release...Do it again...Keep everything else relaxed...Keep breathing...And relax...

Keep breathing...Inhale through your nose...Exhale through your mouth...Inhale...Exhale...

All the tension has left your body...You are completely relaxed...Be aware of your body feeling completely relaxed...peace and total relaxation...Be aware of how your breathing keeps you in a state of relaxation...

Continue to breath slowly...Let yourself float...

Inhale...Exhale...Inhale...Exhale...

(Pause)

When you are ready, stretch and slowly sit up.

If you sit up too quickly, you may feel a lightheadedness. Take it slowly. How does your body feel? Probably different from how it normally feels. Maybe like it feels when you awake from a restful sleep. Some parts of your body may have been easier for you to relax than others. If that is the case for you, practice as often as you can until you're able to achieve total relaxation.

These exercises will decrease your responses to stress, but they will not make stresses go away. To do that usually takes some hard work; here are a few ideas about how to reduce stress in the long run. Since stress is a response **within us**, we first need to recognize that we hold the key within us to mastering stress. Managing stress is part of your personal power, and as that sense of power within yourself increases, so will your ability to manage stress. If stress is a result of your own feeling that you can't quite cope with the events or patterns we talked about earlier, most likely it is because you **learned** to feel powerless earlier in your life.

We **learn** to feel stressed. How does this happen? As we grow up we run into a number of stress situations, some of which we handle all right, and some of which we don't. Some of us are consistently presented with situations that are beyond our abilities or tools to resolve. For example, a parent may have set very high standards, or expected perfection from us; and we might have learned that no matter how hard we try we can't do well enough. We learn to expect to fail. This is especially true if we are often presented with "no win" situations. If a seven-year-old boy watches his father beating his mother, what is his reaction? All kinds of thoughts probably go on inside him. He might want to protect his mother and stop the beating. He might hate his father and wish he could kill him, and know he'd get a severe beating if he tried. He might identify with his father's power and violence, in which case he'd also be likely to feel ashamed of wanting to hurt his mother. He might just turn off and try to ignore the whole thing, giving up hope of having some effect. There is nothing this boy can do to feel good about himself. In situations such as these we come to doubt that we have the personal power to resolve the conflicts of life.

If we learn to be stressed, we can unlearn it as well. To do this we need to set up a new pattern of responding to stress. This might include:

1. Immediate stress reduction, or quieting

2. Assessing realistically what we can and cannot do about the stressful situation

3. Identifying our feeling response to stress

4. Directly discussing the stressful situation and our feelings with others

5. Changing our expectations or guidelines for ourselves, so that we do what we can and let perfection take care of itself

Remember, a crisis that brings on stress is not only an opportunity for disaster. You can use a crisis for positive accomplishment as well — it depends on your interpretation and your sense of personal power.

77

For example, during his tenth session in one of our groups, Carl was excited to tell us about something that had happened to him that week. His seven-year-old son had been hit by a car while out riding his bike. The injury wasn't severe, but Carl and his wife Julie didn't know that at first. Carl and Julie had been working very hard recently at improving their communication. When the accident occurred, Carl felt the stress of worrying about what had happened to his son, and he realized his first impulse was to blame the accident on Julie. He then went on to think about how much his family meant to him, and took some time to reflect on his feelings in the face of this stress. He realized he was frightened of what might have happened to his son, angry at the driver and a little guilty himself that he might have been responsible in some way. He also realized that he expected himself to be an unbending pillar of strength for his family, and that expectation itself was stressful. He was able to discuss his feelings with Julie, and hear her talk about her own feelings (which weren't that different from his). Instead of an angry argument, they found themselves supporting one another. The result of this crisis was that Carl and Julie wound up feeling closer together, and more optimistic about the future.

Think about a stressful event that's recently occurred in your relationship. How could you have used it to your advantage?

Exercise: Managing a Stressful Event

In the space below write down one of the stress events that you checked off earlier. Then list your own steps about how you would manage it — what you could do, and what you couldn't. Be as realistic with yourself as you can. If no one else were influencing you, what expectations would you have of yourself?

Stressful event:_____

What I could do to manage it:_____

_____

My expectations of myself:_____

_____

There is one further way of managing stress. It may seem very simple, but it's surprising how often it simply does not occur to people. Look at your life to see what repeatedly causes you stress and change it! If, for example, you are repeatedly stressed by a boss that you hate, try to talk it out with him, get a transfer or even consider changing jobs — it may be worth it! Certain patterns in your behavior may lead to chronic stress. If you have a tendency to hold in feelings or sidestep assertion, you set yourself up for more stress. Change this pattern! People who are isolated or feel alone often experience greater stress — find ways to increase your contacts and friendships with others. If you are repeatedly caught unprepared by events, make a conscious effort to plan ahead. It's sometimes a great comfort to have "contingency plans." Finally, if your life is all work and no play, you're also more likely to be stressed. Consider setting aside some play time to unwind — hobbies or crafts, working out at the gym, playing softball, or whatever activity fits you.

Exercise: Managing Stressful Patterns

In the space below, write down one or two patterns that cause stress in your life. Then list ways you can think of to change those patterns. Maybe it wouldn't be possible to change them, but write them down anyway. Do they fit into any of the examples given above?

Stressful patterns: _____

Ways I could change those patterns: _____

_____

The Usefulness of Stress

After talking so much about how to reduce or eliminate stress, let's talk about one more aspect of stress: its **usefulness**. Stress may be useful to the part of you that resists change and does not want to expose your vulnerability. Maintaining a constant worry about stressful events may help that more resistant part of you by keeping the focus "out there," blaming the stresses rather than looking inward at your "sore spots." When used this way, stress will prevent you from making needed changes. But it may also protect you from making too many changes too fast. If this is the case for you, you may find that when you try to change the stressful pattern in your life, you make no headway or even experience more stress. So if you try to manage your stress and are consistently unsuccessful, take a look at how stress may be useful or even necessary to "insulate" you in your current way of living.

Dont try for perfection in stress reduction. Do as well as you can for now; with practice you will probably get better. No matter how wonderful they are, **everyone** experiences stress at times.

Study Questions

1. What are the major stressful events you have experienced in the past year of your life?

2. What chronic stress are you currently experiencing?

3. How do you cope with the stress in your life?

4. Complete one or more of the stress coping exercises in this chapter.

5. How could you use a stressful event or chronic stress to your advantage?

6. How has your partner coped with the stress of your violence?

7. How has your approach to coping with stress caused you more stress?

Anger Journal

Date					
Intensity	1 2 3 4 5 6 7 8 9 10		1 2 3 4 5 6 7 8 9 10		
Physical Signs					
Behavior Signs					
Situation					
Did you take a Time-Out?	Yes	No	Yes	No	
	Comments		Comments		
Did you Stuff it, Escalate it, Direct it?	Stuff it	Escalate it	Stuff it	Escalate it	
	Comments	Direct it	Comments	Direct it	
"I" Statements	I'm feeling		I'm feeling		
Physical Activity					
Alcohol or Drug use?	Yes	No	Yes	No	
	Comments		Comments		

CHAPTER TEN

JEALOUSY

In Chapters Seven and Eight we've talked about how to better express what's on your mind, and in your heart, in an intimate relationship. Most of us want intimate relationships to be special, so that we can be ourselves and be appreciated for just who we are. But what happens when we don't feel as special as we think we should? What happens when a partner doesn't follow our expectations, or when others seem more "special" to her than we do?

In this chapter we will look at a problem that comes up at some time for most people, but can be especially severe in abusive relationships. Jealousy — what it is, where it comes from, what you can do about it.

What Is Jealousy?

If you've been jealous, you know that no definition can do justice to jealousy's purely emotional power. A man who's experienced the power of jealousy will usually describe it as a deep fear that his partner will give away to someone else what she's supposed to share only with him. This could be time, attention, or closeness, but the most threatening thing she could give to someone else is usually sex.

When in the grip of sexual jealousy, both men and women may do irrational things they later remember with embarrassment, regret or even shame. They behave as if "possessed" by the jealous fears. The man who takes a day off work to follow his wife around, or who lets the air out of his best friend's tires, may later wonder what made him do it. The man who beats his wife may be even more likely to feel that "something **made** him do it."

Earlier, we discussed the difference between anger and violence: anger is a feeling, and violence is only one way to express that feeling. Jealousy is similar. It is a complex feeling, and there are many ways — choices — to express that feeling as well. In fact, jealous feelings often escalate just as anger does. A man may start out with low level jealous feelings, and perhaps think they are too minor, or silly, or uncomfortable to express. The pressure may build as he begins to think more about them and begins to have jealous fantasies, maybe even quite detailed mental pictures, of what his partner is doing. He may become preoccupied with these jealous thoughts to the point of losing touch with reality. Finally he may believe that he has to do something desperate to make sure his fantasy doesn't happen.

Though he may not be aware of it, he has choices at each step along the way. He can intimidate and threaten his partner, or he can express his feelings directly to her. He can keep to himself with painfully jealous thoughts, or he can talk about them with a close friend or counselor.

Have you experienced jealousy in your past relationships? What kinds of things make you feel jealous? Are there particular jealous fantasies you repeatedly have about your partner? What are your own physical and behavioral signs that may give you "early warning" when jealousy begins to develop?

Exercise: Jealousy

In the exercise below, think about two times in the past that you have felt jealous. For each one write down the incident that made you jealous, your jealous fantasy, and your jealous behavior. For example:

Incident: **My wife got home late from shopping last Tuesday.**

Fantasy: **I was thinking she was out with her divorced friends and might meet someone.**

Jealous behavior: **I took away her car keys, and told her she couldn't have them unless she had a damn good reason.**

1. Incident: _____

_____

Fantasy: _____

_____

Jealous behavior: _____

_____

2. Incident: _____

_____

Fantasy: _____

_____

Jealous behavior: _____

_____

Jealousy and Loss

Most people's jealous fantasies involve fears of loss. Some of these feared losses are actual, but just as frightening are the symbolic losses — the inner meaning of those actual losses. Let's look at an example of how this works.

Jim and Ellen were eagerly awaiting the arrival of their first baby, and both of them expected it would bring a new closeness to their relationship. But after their daughter was born, Ellen spent a great deal of time caring for their baby's physical and emotional needs. Jim felt more and more left out, and found himself angry at Ellen and jealous of his daughter.

Jim actually was losing considerable time and attention from his wife. But what brought out his strong feelings of anger and jealousy was what that **meant** to him. So long as his wife had put him first, he felt emotionally secure. But when another person suddenly was number one, he began to fear he'd lose the sense of security he felt with Ellen. He also felt powerless — he felt his daughter had taken away from him the special relationship with Ellen that he needed, and there was nothing he could do about it.

Jealous fears reflect many different types of potential loss. If a man's partner were to have sex with someone else, he might feel the loss of that special intimate connection that makes him important and secure. He might also be losing face in a social sense if other people found out. His ego or self-esteem might be threatened with questions about whether he's a good enough lover or exciting enough as a person or a good enough provider. He might also lose time and attention he could be sharing with his partner. He might also fear her running away with another man.

All these losses tend to produce the strongest passions in the area of sexual jealousy, but it's important to remember that a man can feel the same jealous fears of his partner's women friends, her work, school, a hobby, or the children. Anything that threatens to deprive him of her exclusive attention or threatens to make her less dependent on him, can cause jealousy.

Sometimes the fear of loss is so strong that we interpret actions based on what we fear, rather than what actually has happened. Think about what you might have been afraid of losing in each of those jealous incidents youve just described. How realistic are these fears? It's often helpful to "reality check" these fears by talking to an objective friend or counselor. What you fear might be true, but quite often it **seems** a lot worse than it **is**.

Why Are We Jealous?

Do you see yourself as a jealous person, or have your partner or other people told you that you are? We believe that some people are more likely than others to develop jealous fears, and this is due to experiences early in life. Two types of people are particularly vulnerable to jealousy: those who have low self-esteem in general, and those who've felt specific losses early in life.

Everyone grows up with some negative messages about himself or herself, coming from parents, relatives, teachers, or others who are important to us. Some people get such consistently negative messages about themselves that they come to believe they are bad and worthless, or at least not good enough. They may not recognize this about themselves most of the time, and may cover up the bad feelings with an outer layer of toughness, exaggerated self-importance, or passive agreeableness.

A person who feels bad about himself often tries to regain some sense of self-worth by being seen as worthy in the eyes of his partner. He cannot really feel good about himself unless he believes his partner is appreciating, or even adoring him. And, he becomes dependent on her for something he can really only provide for himself. It is this dependency that makes him vulnerable to jealousy.

He hopes she will see him as wonderful, but at the same time he fears she will "find out" how worthless he is. If she withdraws her approval he has no **inner** security to fall back on, so he carefully watches for any signs of withdrawal or rejection. He expects abandonment and rejection — after all, he's been rejected enough in the past. So, when she smiles at another man at a party, what he sees is his own insecurity — "He's more attractive than me, I'm not good enough and I'm going to lose her." Jealous fears "take possession" of him — since the fears come from a part of himself he is not aware of, they truly feel foreign, like a "possession" — and he tries to control her behavior to prevent this loss. The usual outcome, of course, is just the opposite of what he wants — she is frightened, pulls back from him emotionally, and thinks less of him.

A similar process takes place for people who've experienced losses early in life, such as the loss of a parent through death or divorce, or loss of the family through placement with other relatives or a foster family. Another loss that a child experiences is one that results from abuse. The child who is physically, sexually or psychologically abused feels a temporary or permanent loss of love from the parent who is abusing him. Likewise, the child who witnesses family violence is also likely to feel abandoned by his parents who are so involved with their own conflict that he gets lost in the process. In either case, the child experiences a feeling of abandonment. Children in alcoholic families are also "abandoned" by parents who are overtaken by their disease and are unable to parent. The prospect of being abandoned — losing a partner's attention and affection — is a direct symbolic reminder of the pain suffered from that earlier loss. Again, a man will try to protect against that deep pain of loss by controlling his partner through threats, intimidation, or even violence. And again, the outcome usually leaves him feeling more abandoned and in more pain than before.

In both these cases sexual jealousy is the most powerful — and painful. In making love there is a blending together with a partner; the boundaries between man and woman seem to dissolve and we feel at one. We enter a partner and give her an emotional part of ourself. When that special connection is threatened the stakes are very high — not only might we lose that person and what she represents, but it's as if a part of our self could be torn out.

A man whose self-worth is shaky, or who fears abandonment, is especially vulnerable to jealousy in battering relationships. This is because a woman who is battered often attempts to cope by withdrawing emotionally and physically from her partner. The man may not understand that it is his violence that is producing this effect, and may interpret her withdrawal as cause for jealousy.

Reflect for a moment on the part your background could play in your jealous feelings. Are you primed for jealous fears by feelings of insecurity or loss? Do you give your partner power over whether you feel good about yourself?

Respecting Personal Boundaries

In this book we keep coming back to the issue of power and control in relationships. That's because it's an important part of jealousy, violence and self-esteem. A key purpose of this book is to help men learn to exercise less control over their partners, and feel more in control of themselves — more secure about their personal boundaries.

Men are raised to feel in control of both themselves and their surroundings. Part of being a man is to make sure that everything around you goes as it should go. This sense of responsibility is noble, though overwhelming, when applied to keeping the ordinary business of life on track. But when we try to extend that responsibility to other people's actions, ideas and inner feelings, we face a truly impossible task. One person cannot control another's inner world, and can control the other's actions only by being intrusive and risking abusive behavior.

When we try to extend our control to another person, we extend our personal boundaries to include the other person as well. A man might merge his boundaries with his partner by taking responsibility for her actions and emotions. He might also blur these personal boundaries by depending on her esteem of him to feel good about himself—giving over an important part of his identity into her hands. The more he depends on her, the more the boundaries between them get unclear. After a while, it gets hard for him to tell where his emotions leave off and hers begin. Not being in control of his own emotional boundaries, he tries to feel safe and in control of himself by being in control of her.

Unless a conscious effort is made to change, this pattern becomes more entrenched. A man may continue to try harder and harder to control his partner, while at the same time feeling more and more insecure. Since he can never control her enough, this will simply not be an effective way for him to feel good about himself.

Another problem with this pattern is that when a relationship with merged boundaries explodes and breaks apart — when the women leaves or gets the man to leave — the man can be vulnerable to unexpectedly deep feelings of loss and aloneness. He may feel despair and hopelessness, as if a part of himself has been taken away. If this is the case for you, it may be especially important for you to use your group, your counselor and your friends to discuss ways of feeling directly in control of you. You may find that taking direct charge of your emotional boundaries leads to increased self-esteem, and decreased feelings of jealousy.

Confronting Jealousy

In confronting jealousy, it is important to acknowledge the purposes it serves, both positive and negative. Let's first look at the positive side. Jealousy helps to mobilize energy to fight for something important when we are **truly** threatened with loss.

If your partner's interest and affection are drifting away from you, if she is increasingly spending time with other friends and activities, then you are threatened with the loss of something important to you and you may want to fight for it. Directly expressing your fear of loss and your anger (directing it) will bring this problem to the surface and will also tell her that you want to solve it. You will be helping build trust, and she may think better of you when she sees that you are working to solve the problems of your relationship in a non-violent way. An uninvolved third person, like a counselor, might also be able to help with this.

But if your partner's attention is moving out into the world, she might not necessarily be preparing to abandon you. She may only be developing her own interests and a sense of independence. Many women today feel a need to create a life outside their home and family. Education, advertising, the media — all offer models of women who pursue interests beyond those of the traditional housewife. At the same time, many women have also been raised with the expectation that they will manage the smooth running of a household. If their outside activities interfere, they often have a sense of guilt and frustration. It is very difficult to fill many roles satisfactorily, as you can appreciate, if you are a husband, lover, father, son, employee, boss and friend.

If you feel dependent on your partner and need her to be dependent on you, if she is somehow necessary for your survival, then it's hard to react calmly to this threat of loss. Actually, as we've discussed before, this reminder of old losses can stir up your emotions even more than an actual loss of your partner's attention. And those stirred-up emotions are likely to interpret her actions in the worst way possible. That smile at another man at a party becomes, in your mind, her intention to have an affair. Her starting a new job means to you that she no longer sees you as a good provider. Then you begin to see jealousy's negative purposes.

We've already mentioned how jealousy can be a way of trying to control your partner when you are feeling insecure and powerless. Jealousy, just like violence, can be a tool to get another person to do what you want. If a partner yields to jealous demands, you may feel reassured (at least temporarily!), and relieved of some fear of loss.

For some people, jealousy is also a way of punishing a partner. It may be a way of getting out your anger about what she has actually done to you, or what you expect she will do. In fact, you may wind up punishing her for things **other** people have done to you, perhaps long in the past.

Another function of jealousy is that it keeps a partner at a distance even while you seem to demand closeness. The very nature of jealousy is to armor yourself and keep your more vulnerable feelings well protected. You can take a superior stand, demanding that she be completely open and trusting with you, but clearly saying you don't trust her. The end result is that jealousy destroys trust for both of you.

Taking Charge of Your Jealousy

Because it's so complex, jealousy is usually difficult to work out on your own. But there are some things you can do, beyond talking with your partner about your jealous feelings, to decrease the problems that jealousy causes. When you are under stress, jealous fears are more likely to come bursting out. When you are feeling good about yourself, jealousy feels more in perspective. So, prevention is important.

The exercises in Chapter 9 will help you to lower your level of stress. Directing your feelings with your partner, as we discussed in Chapter 4, will help to keep jealousy from escalating. You can also avoid putting yourself in situations that will make you jealous. And when that isn't possible, you can try to anticipate those situations and rehearse within yourself more positive ways of reacting.

Are your jealous fears related to your own insecurity or to a dependent need for your partner? Then you need to work at getting your sense of self-worth and power from within yourself, rather than looking just to your partner for approval. We recognize that many people will be cautious about pulling back from dependency with a partner: "If she doesn't need me all the time, and I don't need her, what will keep us together?" But relationships **based** on dependency usually come apart in time. A loving, trusting respect for one another is a much better glue in the long run. And if you can make your security more independent of another person, you have the payoff of lowered stress and anxiety, increased self-control, and greater self-esteem.

As couples examine their dependent needs of one another, they may also become aware that there is a sense of ownership in a relationship — especially the man's sense of owning his wife or partner. It wasn't so very long ago that society clearly believed that a man possessed his wife as property and was responsible for her behavior. Those times are past, but many men still carry an attitude of ownership with a partner. In order to let go of jealousy, you may need to remind yourself that your partner **really is** her own person, and responsible for her own behavior.

Lastly, you may just try asking yourself if this jealousy is realistic? Does your jealous behavior contribute in a positive or a negative way to your relationship and your self-esteem? Remember, **you** are in control of your own behavior and can choose what **you** will do when your jealous feelings threaten to take over.

Study Questions

1. What are your jealousies in your current relationship?

2. How do you show your jealousy?

3. What makes you particularly vulnerable to jealousy?

4. How do you use your jealousy to control your partner?

5. What would happen if you stopped controlling your partner?

Anger Journal

Date		
Intensity	1 2 3 4 5 6 7 8 9 10	1 2 3 4 5 6 7 8 9 10
Physical Signs		
Behavior Signs		
Situation		
Did you take a Time-Out?	Yes / No Comments	Yes / No Comments
Did you Stuff it, Escalate it, Direct it?	Stuff it / Escalate it Comments / Direct it	Stuff it / Escalate it Comments / Direct it
"I" Statements	I'm feeling	I'm feeling
Physical Activity		
Alcohol or Drug use?	Yes / No Comments	Yes / No Comments

CHAPTER ELEVEN

CHANGING PATTERNS WITH YOUR PARTNER

Over one-half of the women who are being battered by their partners resort to separation or divorce as a means to protect themselves from the violence. In at least half of these cases the woman will return to give the relationship, and her partner, another chance.

Through our experience working with men in groups, we have found that many men have difficulty applying what they learned in the group session to their home situation. Sometimes saying that you feel angry in group, to a stranger, is much easier than saying it to your lover. In group there is usually a facilitator or mediator who helps the communication process stay on track. At home you are face-to-face with your partner, without that outside, objective observer who can support you both in talking about difficult feelings. Communication can wander off into areas where there are old hurts and angers. Even with the best intentions, communications can get more confused and add on more problems. To help keep you on the right track, we suggest that couples who are interested in staying together receive couples counseling, once the man learns to control his anger.

Many of the wives of the men in our groups want to know what it is they can do to help their partners stop the violence. Our answer is,

"You cannot make your partner stop his violence; all you can do is openly support him in his efforts. However, you **can** find ways of helping yourself overcome the anger and hurt that you feel as a result of his violence."

In order to accomplish this, we suggest that women receive counseling too — to learn new ways of communicating their own anger, and to heal the emotional wounds from violence. In addition, through individual or couples counseling a man and a woman can learn new ways of communicating with each other. For when a man stops his violent behavior, it creates a new atmosphere in the house. There is less tension and, in particular, less fear of expressing feelings. For some couples, this freedom in expressing themselves leads them into unknown territory. "Can I really communicate my feelings to him?" "How can I get her to understand what it is I am feeling inside?" To find the answers to these questions both the man and the woman must be patient and committed to working through a confusion of conflicting feelings — vulnerability and defensiveness, love and anger, fear, rejection and dependent need. Understanding another person is so easy in theory, but so difficult in practice.

The purpose of this chapter is to help you begin to look at how you and your partner communicate and try out some new patterns of communication. If you are currently separated from your partner, or already divorced, you may still want to complete these exercises. You may want to work with a friend, lover, family member, counselor or a member of your men's group. The exercises are not just for your partner or your relationship, they are for **You!**

Non-Verbal Communication

Throughout this book we have emphasized communicating your feelings with words. But, words are not the only way to say what we feel inside. In fact, people are often not aware that they are communicating their feelings, because they communicate those feelings non-verbally. Research has shown that much of what we communicate is not done verbally, but through our body. The face, in particular, is quite expressive of inner emotions, while the body communicates the intensity of those feelings. In Chapter Four we talked about how anger is often expressed in this way without using words.

Anger is probably one of the more difficult emotions for men or women to deal with effectively. Most of us were taught as children that getting angry was the equivalent to being out of control. Or often, a child who is abused may have to hold back his anger, and carry secrets, in order to protect himself from further abuse and protect the guilty parent. If our parents didn't give us the opportunity to openly express our angry feelings, we may have grown up to avoid situations that make us feel angry or may try to cover up our anger. Many people are so out of touch with their feelings they may not even be aware when they are feeling anger.

Sadness is another feeling that people have difficulty expressing. One night in our group Dave appeared, looking like he'd lost his best friend. When each man was asked how he felt, Dave said, " I'm feeling fine." Everyone looked at each other with amazement. "No way you are feeling fine, man," said one of his fellow group members. "Miserable is written all over your face." Dave argued, "No really, I am doing fine." The subject was dropped until Dave shared about his week: "My wife left me Monday."

Dave eventually expressed his sadness and anger verbally. His facial and body expressions had **sad** written all over them, and others saw the feelings in him before he could see them himself. He was communicating feelings to the other men in the group, quite powerfully, even before he could use words to describe them.

We may be communicating a particular emotion, or the others may only see that some strong feelings are going on inside us and may not be aware of what they are. What happens when your partner says, "Honey, what's wrong, you seem upset?" Do you feel open and willing to talk about your troubles, or is it important to show her that you're fine? Sometimes the more a woman asks about his feelings, the more a man will insist that everything is OK. It is not unusual that someone else will be able to see our feelings expressed in body language or behavior before we are aware of them ourselves. Unfortunately, many men may take this questioning by a partner as an invasion or attack. We may need to learn to trust that others can see feelings in us before we are aware of those feelings ourselves.

Just as you may be unaware of your feelings, or that you're communicating them, your partner may receive your communication without being aware of it. Non-verbal communication works that way — messages are given and received, and even acted upon, without conscious awareness. Your partner **might** be thinking "His anger is building, he might explode, I'd better protect myself"; but she might instead be feeling tense, uncomfortable and headachy and not know why. You might sense her getting distant from you, and you will act based on what you think she is feeling, without knowing for sure what is really going on inside of her. In an escalating conflict, lack of awareness of our non-verbal communication can be dangerous.

The following exercise is to be completed non-verbally and without touching each other.

Exercise: Non-Verbal Communication Part 1

Sit face to face with your partner at about arm's length. The woman goes first and the man observes.

Without words, tell him that you are feeling angry. Express your anger in your face and your body. Take about a minute. Let him look you over and observe your facial and body expressions.

Now the man expresses his anger without words, and the woman observes.

Repeat the exercise. Without words, take turns to tell your partner that you are feeling sad. Show your feelings in your face and your body. Take a minute. Just observe the facial and body expressions.

Repeat the exercise one more time. Non-verbally tell each other that you are feeling afraid.

Try other feelings such as happiness, confusion, sexy, nervous, tired, etc. A certain amount of playfulness may be possible here — "Name that Feeling."

The next part of this exercise involves some talking.

Exercise: Non-Verbal Communication Part 2

Sit face to face with your partner at about arm's length. This time the man goes first.

Look at your partner's face and body. What feelings do you see in her? Be careful! Don't tell her what you want her to feel or what you're afraid she is feeling, but look very closely; what feelings do you see her showing you with her face and body. Tell her what you see. Be sure to begin your statement, "I see you feeling..."

She just has to listen. No correction, no feedback, no talking. Even if he is wrong, just listen and take it in. When he is finished, tell him "Thank you."

Now change roles. The woman looks at his face and body and tells him what she sees. When she is finished, he tells her "Thank you."

This seems like a simple exercise, but it is difficult in practice. It takes good observation skills and a willingness to look and act a little silly. Go back and try these exercises several times. You might be amazed at how much better you can get to know your partner and yourself.

Developing Your Listening Skills

Let's listen in on the beginning of a major argument between Bob and Alice.

Alice: You never call when you are going be late coming home.

Bob: What about the time you invited your parents over when I was supposed to go to the ball game?

Alice: You'll do anything to avoid my family!

Bob: You're always on my case! Can't you give me some slack?

Alice: What about you? You....

Sounds familiar? Each attack or response in this conversation seems, to the outside listener, almost completely unrelated to what went before it. It's as if Bob and Alice are talking to one another, but not listening while they're doing it. Can you remember any of your own arguments that have begun like this and escalated to violence? By applying what you have learned so far in this book, you can prevent this escalation. Let's analyze some of the problems in Bob and Alice's few comments to each other.

Right from the start Alice accuses Bob of something. Accusations such as this are bound to put anyone on the defensive. She uses the word "never," which is a very loaded word. It falls into the same category as "always," and "every time" — words that suggest that there are no deviations from a pattern, no exceptions to the rule, and no way to escape the accusation. Our experience with human behavior is that people rarely **always** or **never** do anything. And including "always" or "never" in a critical comment is a sure way to turn criticism into attack, and challenge your partner to defend him or herself. Perhaps Alice may have wanted to begin by directing her feelings instead.

Alice: I feel angry that you didn't call me tonight to tell me that you were going to be late.

Bob's response is a common defensive strategy: he takes the heat off himself by shifting the blame to Alice. He doesn't respond to Alice's point, he responds instead to her anger and his own fear that she will get "one up" on him. Of course Alice will respond to his challenge and continue to escalate the argument. Had he paused for a minute, he might have said to himself something like this;

Bob (to himself): She sounds like she is angry at me. I guess she may have a point there. It makes me angry when she invites her family and doesn't tell me.

Deliberating before you respond can be one of the most effective ways of learning to listen to and understand your partner. Give yourself a minute, then respond to what you hear her trying to say, before you bring up your own complaints and issues. This will keep the conversation from escalating into an intense argument. Bob may respond to her in the following way;

Bob: OK, I can understand why you feel angry at the fact that I didn't call last night. I will call you when I am going to be late.

Bob may also want to communicate his feelings. He may be feeling bad that she is upset with him. He may be feeling angry because he doesn't think he has to call her. He may be feeling afraid that she may be rejecting him. Or he may not know why he is feeling sad or angry himself. However, when he communicates his feelings in a direct, non-intimidating manner Alice can better respond to him.

Bob: I feel bad right now. I guess I'm afraid that you are telling me that you don't love me or I am bad.

Alice: Of course I love you. That's why it upsets me when you don't call. I look forward to seeing you at the end of the day.

Bob (to himself): She's telling me that she loves me. That makes me feel better.

Bob (to Alice): That makes me feel better.

Of course this is an ideal outcome of this conversation. Most of us fall into a category somewhere in between, but probably closer to the first example. We tend to listen to our fears of what the other person is saying, rather than what she is actually saying. The following exercise is a way you can avoid the escalation trap. It will give you experience at learning to **listen** and **respond** to your partner rather than **react** to her.

Exercise: Listening

The following is an exercise we recommend both in our groups when men are communicating with each other, and at home when they are trying to communicate with their partners.

Make an agreement with your partner that for one night this week you will completely change your pattern of communicating so that what you have to say to each other will go through the following five steps.

1. The speaker will state clearly what he wants to say, using "I" statements.

2. The listener will repeat what he or she has just heard the other person say, in detail.

3. The speaker will then confirm what the listener has heard, and then repeat whatever important points the listener did not hear.

4. The listener is then to repeat this back until the speaker is satisfied that he or she heard everything. Only then can the listener respond.

5. Now the roles reverse, and the new listener repeats what he or she heard until the speaker is satisfied.

Below is an example of how such a conversation may sound to the outside observer:

Rick: I have something to tell you in our new way of communicating.

Sue: OK.

Rick: The other day when we were at your mother's house you made some comment about my taking Time-Outs so much that we hardly spend any time with each other these days. I felt angry at the time but I stuffed it because I was afraid of taking a Time-Out. I know that wasn't your fault, but I want you to know that maybe we aren't spending time together, but it's better than before.

Sue: OK. I heard you say that you were angry when I told my mother about you taking too many Time-Outs and that we hardly spend any time together. Right?

Rick: Is that all?

Sue: Yes.

Rick: I also said that I stuffed it and I wanted to take a Time-Out then but I was afraid. I also said that it wasn't your fault, and I know we haven't spent much time together these days, but it's better than before.

Sue: You said that you stuffed it at the time and you know that wasn't my fault. Let's see, what else did you say? Oh yes, you said that you know that we don't spend time together, but you think it's better than when you were violent. Something like that. Did I get it?

Rick: Right.

Sue: Can I respond now?

Rick: Sure.

Sue: I feel good that you're telling me about this clearly. But I also feel angry about something. Maybe it's that when you take so many Time-Outs I feel you're running away from me and wanting to spend less time with me.

Rick then has to repeat to Sue what she has communicated. Sue is to keep repeating what she has said until Rick gets it right. This type of communication is tedious, but it's only one night a week and it gives you a chance to actually hear what your partner is saying to you — and know that what you have to say is also heard. By listening you can avoid reacting, escalating and possibly saying or doing something you later regret.

Making Contact at the End of the Day

Each couple seems to have a time during the day when they fight the most. Most frequently arguments occur at the end of the work day when one or both people return home. For you, it may be at dinner, just before going to bed or when you wake up in the morning. Whenever your high risk times are, you can incorporate certain rituals in your day to day living that make it less likely these explosions will occur. One such ritual is called "Connection Time." The purpose of this exercise is for couples to connect in a positive way at the end of the day. You may do it when you both get home from work. You may want to wait until the kids are asleep or when you are about to sit down to dinner. It is good to agree on a consistent time every day so there are no miscommunications about when the exercise will be done. Decide who is going to speak first. That person has five minutes to talk about anything he wants; work, friends, family, sex, the grass that needs mowing, the basement that needs to get cleaned — whatever you want to talk about (excluding psychological violence, of course). It is a time to talk about whatever it is that's important to you without being interrupted.

The other person is just to listen; no reactions, no responses, just listen and take it in. If you can't fill up the five minutes, sit together and look into each other's eyes or sit side by side in silence. You can do whatever you want with your five minutes just as long as you are doing it to connect with your partner. After the five minutes, the listener is to say, "Thank you."

Then switch roles. The new speaker now has five minutes to talk about whatever he wants. When that person is finished, the listener says, "Thank you."

Now switch roles again, but this time the speaker says three things he likes about the other person. These could be things that the person did today or last week. It could be a general thing you like about the other person. When you finish the listener once again says, "Thank you" and you switch roles.

This exercise is another chance to try out a different pattern of communication in your relationship. Clear communication usually doesn't occur unless people make a concerted effort. If it's mostly left to chance, it won't happen. Making an effort to have an intimate connection with your partner is going to feel awkward at first. But it gets easier over time — and don't forget, it doesn't always have to be serious. Make it fun for yourself.

The Dinner Time Ritual

Dave, a member of our group told us about a ritual he and his wife had whenever they would sit down to dinner. He said that if they did it they would never argue. When they didn't do it they often got into some kind or argument or disagreement. He told us,

> "When I was a kid, I remember my father always getting upset at the dinner table. I couldn't digest my food so I would always walk away with an upset stomach. I want to put all the bullshit aside until we finish dinner or solve it beforehand. My wife agrees, so we make dinner a time when we feed each other good emotions as well as good food."

Once the food is on the plate, before eating, everyone at the table would hold hands and close their eyes and be silent for a minute. It is another way of connecting with the family without words. For Dave this was an alternative to the before-dinner prayer. It had more meaning to him and his family than saying a prayer. And it worked for them!

Starting Your Own Ritual

Talk with your partner about developing a ritual for connecting, to use every day or every week. Something that is meaningful for both of you and that helps you feel better about yourselves and each other. This ritual may be taking a walk; it may be reading to each other; it may just be holding hands and sitting next to each other. Your ritual may include your children, friends or other family members. Rituals are important because they create a sense of continuity in your life. It is something you can count on. Jim's ritual of having a Sunday brunch picnic with his wife reminded him of the importance of his relationship. It was a time when he only thought of his wife and himself. He didn't think of work, neighbors, the house or anything else. No matter how difficult his week was he would look forward to Sunday brunch in the park.

Learning from Each Other

So often we hear how men and women are so different. They have different expectations about relationships. Women are always wanting to relate, communicate, talk about their feelings. Men don't want to talk about things all the time, are satisfied just being there, don't know how to express their inner feelings. Women seem to know instinctively how to cook, clean and care for the children. Men automatically know what to do with a hammer and pliers. Women want to make love and men want to have sex. Men and women are different in many ways. But each individual man or woman has both masculine and feminine qualities, and in fact there is a large area of overlap where men and women have qualities in common. For example, is eagerness to learn a masculine or feminine quality? We sometimes talk about the differences between men and women as if they were biologically determined, carved in stone and the root of all problems in intimate relationships. This is not so.

Heredity does play a role in determining what it means to be a man or a woman. But although a large amount of research has been done, no one can say for sure whether certain "feminine" or "masculine" characteristics are absolutely genetically determined. It seems likely that the biggest reason for male-female differences is that men and women learn different skills throughout their lives. Some of these skills developed from the different ways men and women were treated as children. For example, as children, boys learn less about relationships because they are frequently encouraged to be independent and out there in the world, more than girls. On the other hand, girls usually spend more time with mother, other adults or other children than boys. They learn more about relationships through those interactions. Girls learn about personal relationships while boys are learning about group sports or activities. These differences don't have to lead to problems in relationships. They can actually enhance an intimate relationship. How does this work?

We can learn from a partner how to develop those parts of ourselves that are less developed. Steve, a member of our group, had been separated from his partner for six weeks. He was living on TV dinners and fast-food drive-ins. A woman friend of his, Nancy, called him one night to invite him over for a home-cooked meal in exchange for his repairing some things in her house. She was recently divorced and had depended on her husband to fix things around the house. This exchange happened a number of times over six months. One night they were both expressing how amazed they were that the other person just naturally knew how to fix, in his case, and cook, in her case. After talking for a while, Steve realized that he didn't naturally develop his skills, he used to help his father fix things around his house. He had to learn. Nancy realized that she also has spent a great deal of time learning how to cook.

Until then Steve would usually fix things while Nancy was cooking. They decided to change their pattern. They decided that the next time he came over he would watch her cook and she would watch him fix. He learned things he had never known like how to make home-made salad dressing and how to know when the fish was finished baking. After dinner she watched him repair a lamp and change the needle on her stereo. Each of them could see that what the other was doing wasn't quite so mysterious after all.

96

Steve and Nancy were friends, and they were clear that they didn't want any other kind of relationship with each other. Because of their friendship they were able to learn from each other without feeling defensive or feeling put-down by the other person. This kind of learning can also happen in an intimate relationship. It takes trust that the other person cares and is not out to make you feel bad about yourself — an "open" attitude to the other person. What can I learn from this person?

Exercise: What Can you Learn from Each Other?

What can you learn from your partner? Make a list of the areas where your partner is more skilled than you are. What qualities does she or he possess that are in short supply for you? For example:

Debbie is a better cook than me.

She is better at expressing her feelings than I am.

John is better at fixing things around the house than me.

He is better at saying **no** to family than I am.

What skill can **you** learn from your partner? _____

_____

Can you find a way to **help** each other with these skills? _____

_____

_____

For example:

I'm going to watch Debbie next time she cooks.

Next time John is feeling something we are going to sit down, and I will let him tell me his feelings in the best way he knows how. I'll watch his non-verbal expression and tell him what feeling it looks like. I'll try to be patient.

Next time I fix something around the house I'm going to ask if Debbie wants to watch me.

Before I agree to any family activities I am going to talk with John to see if he and I both want to participate. If not, I'm going to practice saying **no** with him and then clearly say **no** to the family.

In addition to skills, you can learn to develop some of your own personal qualities. For example, is your partner more expressive of his or her emotions, more patient, more affectionate, more intellectual, more conscious of his or her physical health, more compassionate, less inhibited, more relaxed? Frequently, we choose partners because they complement our qualities. Dave was a very quiet individual who had a great deal of trouble expressing his feelings. June, his partner, was outgoing and very expressive of her feelings. Those qualities that were initially attractive to him became a source of their problems. As he developed his ability to express his emotions and became more comfortable in group situations, he became more tolerant of those qualities in June. On the other hand, June was very attracted to Dave's attention to details. Yet, her impatience and his slow pace became a frequent point of contention. As she learned to feel comfortable with her own ability to focus on details and slow down, she had an easier time with that part of Dave.

Learning from each other can be one of the most difficult skills a couple can master with each other. Be patient. Like cooking and fixing, it takes time and consistent practice.

Study Questions

1. Try the various exercises in this chapter with your partner. What were your experiences in completing the exercises?

2. What are your communication difficulties in your relationship? Where do you need to improve?

3. What are the qualities in your partner that attracted you to her initially? How do these same qualities cause difficulty for you?

4. What scares you the most about getting close to your partner? What would happen if you really let her get close to you?

5. Do any of the patterns or fears in your current relationship have parallels from your own family?

6. What negative patterns would you like to change in your relationship?

7. What positive patterns or characteristics would you like to see develop or keep if they are already present?

Anger Journal

Date		
Intensity	1 2 3 4 5 6 7 8 9 10	1 2 3 4 5 6 7 8 9 10
Physical Signs		
Behavior Signs		
Situation		
Did you take a Time-Out?	Yes / No — Comments	Yes / No — Comments
Did you Stuff it, Escalate it, Direct it?	Stuff it / Escalate it — Comments / Direct it	Stuff it / Escalate it — Comments / Direct it
"I" Statements	I'm feeling	I'm feeling
Physical Activity		
Alcohol or Drug use?	Yes / No — Comments	Yes / No — Comments

CHAPTER TWELVE

WHAT IF SHE LEAVES?

Separation is a fact of life for physically violent relationships. We've talked about the emotional distance that grows between partners when there is violence. As violence and threats of violence continue, the woman is likely to become more and more emotionally distant, coldly angry, hurt — and unable to express it. She may mistakenly feel guilty herself for the violence, and withdraw in shame. This growing emotional distance is very likely to eventually result in physical separation. Perhaps she will leave during an episode of violence, and find a women's shelter, relative or friend to stay with. Perhaps she will insist at some point that the man move out. The separation may be impulsive and emotional or carefully and rationally thought out, but in fact a large percentage of violent relationships do go through at least temporary separations. The purpose of this chapter is to give you information and guidance that can help you weather the pain and confusion that go along with the loss.

Stages of Separation

Separation doesn't "just happen." Occasionally a woman will separate from her partner after a first episode of violence. We have heard several women say that they felt taking this strong stand — that they would not tolerate violence, and the man needed to change his behavior — made it unlikely their partner would try violence again. More often, physical separation is preceded by **emotional separation**. If the man is surprised by it, it's because he has ignored the signs leading up to separation.

There are different patterns of separation; each couple does it their own way. Emotional separation, brief crisis-oriented separation, longer-term planned separation, separation with or without working plans to reconcile — all these may be mixed together in an individual way for any given couple. Separation may progress to divorce, but even then it may not be complete until years later, when the man and woman truly establish their own identities and let go of their needs for each other.

The **initial physical separation** is likely to be a time of conflict and confusion for each partner. It is also a dangerous time, when violence may escalate. Before the actual separation, it's likely there will have been increasingly poor communication between the man and woman. Out of fear of his violence, she may not have discussed her increasing desperation and need for distance. He may not have told her about his increasing fears of losing her, out of fear that if they talked about it she would indeed leave. They might both be walking on eggs, trying to avoid talking about anything that would make them confront the seriousness of their situation. After the separation, all the held-in fears and angers may come out — she may seem to him to be "surprisingly" angry and rejecting; he may be telling his friends how "unfair" it feels, and how angry and hurt he is. He may desperately try to get her back, partly so that he won't feel lost and out of control. He may alternately try to bully and appease her, so that she will feel more confused and therefore susceptible to his control. He may threaten to harm himself or her, or those who are sheltering her, so she will see how "serious" he is. He may try to intimidate her through increased violence or threats of violence. All these are ways to try to control her behavior and cope with his own feelings of being out of control.

As **separation lengthens,** each person will have the opportunity to begin to look at himself or herself as a separate individual. Each will be able to take a close look at the relationship and determine whether or not it is possible to rebuild trust and to reconcile. She will be watching to see if he is seriously hearing her need to put an end to the violence. He will have the opportunity to look honestly at his patterns of violence, without blaming or denying. He may continue to try to convince her to return, and in their conversations may focus almost exclusively on pleading, reasoning, intimidating or cajoling to get her back. This may help him avoid the discomfort of seeing himself as separate individual. But for true reconciliation to take place, he will need to step back and see her as a separate person who will make her own decision without his control.

If they decide to reconcile, they will try to begin clearer communication, make agreements about their differences, and establish ground rules for a new relationship. One or both of them may be too accommodating and not respect his or her own individual needs. We believe that when partners in a violent relationship attempt to reconcile, it is essential that the man seek counseling, **and** demonstrate clear evidence of change in his behavior before resuming their relationship.

Divorce

Many relationships go through several separations as they try to work through their conflicts and establish a clear sense of individuality for each partner. If ongoing problems cannot be resolved, or if one or both partners give up on the relationship, they enter the next stage of separation — **divorce.** Reconciling the relationship is clearly no longer possible, and both partners are faced with the new task of letting go of something that may once have been the center of their lives. As we've discussed in other chapters, coping with loss can be very painful. A man is likely to feel terribly guilty, to question his self-worth, to feel angry at himself and his partner, to think obsessively about "might-have- beens," to feel empty and alone, and maybe to despair of ever being able to reconstruct a meaningful life for himself. He may become determined to figure out what it was he could have done (or what **she** should have done!) to make everything all right. He may even deny to himself and others that the loss is occurring! All of these are parts of the grieving process: ways of coping with the deep sadness of loss. Eventually he will need to move on to an acceptance of the death of the relationship, letting it go and living his own life. He will need to acknowledge both the positive and negative parts of the relationship, accept responsibility for his wrongs, make amends, and forgive his partner her wrongs. This is a tall order, and his tendency will be to hold on to what **was** by not following through these steps.

The final stage in separation usually doesn't occur until some time after divorce. It often takes a lot longer than the legal six months or year for a man to accept that he is a truly **separate individual.** This does not mean growing cold and uncaring toward an ex-partner (which might actually be a sign of holding on). It does mean recognizing who your partner is as an individual, letting go of your emotional needs from her, and establishing your own independent life.

101

If there are children involved, it will mean working out an agreement in which each parent is respectful of the other's parenting style and is even able to consult together about important parenting issues. It can provide a great sense of accomplishment to have worked through these difficult and painful stages of separation, and achieve an accepting, respectful relationship with an ex-partner.

Exercise: Separation Process

What stage of separation are you in?

1. Emotional separation

2. Initial crisis separation

3. Longer-term separation

4. Legal divorce

5. Emotional divorce

Describe how you cope with this separation. For example, how do you try to control her behavior, deal with feelings of loss, guilt or anger?

Describe yourself as an individual, apart from your partner. List your characteristics, what you like to do, what's important in your life.

In the same way, describe your partner as an individual. Step back and look at her as clearly as you can. Recognize the areas where you fit together well, and where you don't.

The Healing Process of Separation

As we've talked about separation so far, each stage has its own problems and also its own potential for healing. But there is one "secret ingredient" that can help heal the wounds in all stages of separation — letting go. Letting go means recognizing that no matter how much you try, you are powerless over your partner's feelings and what she chooses to do with them. It does not mean being cold and distant from her, or that you don't care whether you have a relationship with her or not. But it means letting go of your attempts to control her thinking, her feelings and her behavior. Because letting go is respectful of her individuality, and yours too, it forms the basis of a truly supportive and understanding relationship. Letting go is risky — if you no longer try to control her, she may indeed leave for good. But remember, she needs time and physical distance from you to heal her wounds. You can't heal them for her. **And you can't heal your own wounds if you're holding on to her for dear life.**

Another important healing ingredient is getting help. Men often feel a reluctance to ask for help, especially in those personal areas where they "should" be able to solve their own problems. But asking others for help — your group, counselor, close friend or family member — allows you to let down some of your barriers and thus begin to heal. If you can talk honestly and directly with others about your feelings during the separation, you will take some of the burden off the relationship. When you can't get support from your partner, talking directly with others can provide needed support and help relieve some of the tension and stress of carrying your emotions alone.

As the healing occurs during separation, the problems separating a couple may be resolved and mended. But the real healing and mending needs to occur within each partner as an individual. The man can come back to his partner saying and doing all the "right" things, and she may still choose to end the relationship. The **value** of separation and divorce is that it can provide information and motivation for him to make important changes in how he lives his **own** life. Separation requires him to step back, look at himself as an individual and really assess whether he's living the kind of life he wants. Letting go, asking for help, expressing feelings directly, changing your behavior: these are the healing steps that can enable you to emerge from your separation stronger, and more in possession of yourself, than before.

Exercise: Healing the Separation

1. **Letting go.** What are the ways you can step back from trying to control your partner's behavior? How can you communicate to her that you are letting go? What are your fears of what might happen if you let go?

2. **Asking for help.** Who could you ask for help? What inner barriers or resistances would get in the way of asking? How do you imagine that person would respond if you asked?

3. **Communicate feelings.** Describe your feelings about the separation. What would be the most important feeling to express? If you talked directly about that feeling, how would the person you asked for help respond?

4. **Changing behavior.** What behavior on your part has contributed to the separation? Are you comfortable with that behavior as part of your life? Pick one specific behavior that you don't like and develop a realistic, day-to-day plan to change it. Use your "helping person" to help you develop this plan.

The Next Relationship

It's an old saying that those who don't learn from their mistakes are doomed to repeat them. The most common mistake as a relationship ends is to blame the ex-partner for everything that went wrong. The next most common mistake is to immediately find another mate who is going to do everything "right" that your ex did "wrong." By taking the focus off yourself and your own healing process, you make it much more likely that in your next relationship you will play out the same themes as your last one.

Take it slow. Give yourself time to reflect on your wrongs and review what's important about you as an individual. As you look for your next relationship, remember there's no such thing as a perfect partner. The fantasy person who is going to make everything all right for you, fill all your needs, is just that — a fantasy. It's more important to find a relationship where you can be comfortably who you are, showing both your strengths and weaknesses. It's often best to talk directly at the beginning about your violence. Continue taking

Time-Outs and working on your communication exercises. Even with a new partner, you are still at risk of violence since it is **your** pattern.

Study Questions

1. Has your attempt to cope with separation been successful? How has it succeeded and how hasn't it?

2. What has been difficult about letting go of your partner during your separation?

3. What have you learned about yourself during this separation?

4. Select another group member to be your "helping person." Call him up during the next week and discuss how you could make specific changes in a part of your life that you don't like.

5. Discuss three of your characteristics that you would like to change before resuming your relationship, or beginning a new one.

CHAPTER THIRTEEN

WHERE TO GO FROM HERE

Now that you have almost completed *Learning to Live Without Violence*, it's time to begin to think about what you have learned and where you need go next. As we have mentioned earlier, old habits die hard. Unless you continue to consciously examine your anger and other feelings every day, you are likely to act them out in one one of your old patterns, such as violence or substance abuse.

The exercises in this book were not written to solve all the problems in your relationship. Our goal has been to help you, either by yourself or with the aid of counseling, learn new ways to handle anger and other feelings. In order to make sure that what you have learned stays in place, we strongly recommend that some weekly support continue for some period of time. For this reason, we believe that weekly counseling is especially important at this time. You are trying to change a pattern of your behavior, and like other habits, that pattern will resist change. Counseling will provide support and some increased understanding of yourself that will help you to continue in the direction you want to go.

Another reason for counseling is that as you change, your communication with your partner must also change. It is difficult to adjust to new ways of communicating. Therefore, some guidance may be helpful. If you do not change the ways you communicate with your partner, or if you just cannot communicate, you risk returning to a pattern of violence.

How to Find Effective Counseling

Many of the men who come to our program tell us they haven't had an easy time finding help for this problem. In this chapter we've written out some of our ideas on the subject of finding a counselor. We hope this will be helpful to you. In addition, you may be interested in starting a self-help program in your area. In the appendix we offer suggestions on how to go about setting up such a group in your community.

Counseling Defined

Throughout this workbook, we have used the words counselor or counseling. Because we are mental health professionals, it is sometimes easy for us to take for granted that all people know what we mean when we use these words. Lets begin with a few definitions.

Counsel: mutual exchanging of ideas, opinions, etc.; discussion and deliberation

Counseling: 1. to give advice; to advise. 2. to recommend; urge the acceptance of an action, plan, etc.

Counselor: a person who counsels; advisor

Basically, a counselor is an advisor, a person who can help someone develop a plan of action for change. In this case, we are talking about helping someone change so that he is no longer violent.

Types of Counselors

If you look at a list of counselors you will see titles or degrees after their names. These titles or degrees will tell you something about a professional's training, and the counseling approach that he or she may take. Basically, there are six types of counselors:

1. Marriage, Family and Child Counselor (M.A., M.F.C.C.)

2. Peer Counselor

3. Psychiatrist (M.D.)

4. Licensed Psychologist (Ph.D.)

5. Religious Counselor

6. Licensed Clinical Social Worker (M.S.W., L.C.S.W.)

Marriage, Family and Child Counselors are generally taught to deal with problems of marriage or relationships. They also may work with children. They are usually concerned with the whole family and will often see them all together. They also work with couples, individuals and groups.

Peer counselors may or may not have any professional training, but their strength lies in their personal experience or personal interest in a particular problem. Peer counselors often work in the fields of child abuse, suicide prevention, and alcohol or drug abuse. There are a number of programs across the country that use a peer counseling approach. Peer counselors usually work with groups or individuals, but can also work with couples and families.

Psychiatrists are medical doctors and are primarily concerned with the study and treatment of disorders of the mind. They can prescribe drugs for more severe mental problems such as depression, psychosis, alcoholism or drug addiction. They may also work within or in conjunction with a medical center, for those persons who need hospitalization. Psychiatrists usually work with individuals and groups, but may also work with couples and families.

Psychologists deal strictly with human behavior and study the causes of behavior, and how to change it through a variety of techniques called psychotherapy. Psychologists can not prescribe medication. They usually work with individuals, but can also work with groups, couples and families.

Religious Counselors are usually priests, ministers, pastors or rabbis. They help people live out the teachings of their particular faith. Their counseling usually has a religious orientation, and they typically see people for a few sessions and then make a referral to a community agency. A member of the clergy is often the first person a man or woman may talk with about this problem. Religious counselors usually see individuals and sometimes couples. They may also lead groups.

Social Workers. Historically, social workers are active members of the community, helping to improve the quality of life in that community. They are usually aware of resources that people may utilize for a particular problem. The social worker works with individuals, couples, families and groups. Like other mental health professionals they are trained to help individuals experiencing problems, like domestic violence.

Approaches to Counseling

The above descriptions are very general. We don't want to imply that all psychiatrists only prescribe drugs, or all social workers use community resources, or all religious counselors refer to religion alone. Counseling is a very individualistic occupation. Most of us professionals feel a little uncomfortable if someone pins a label on us and tries to say **that** is who we are. We usually branch out from our basic areas of training, taking some ideas and methods from one field, some from another, until we build an approach that works best for us.

In this way, several different styles of counseling have evolved out of different theories of what makes people work. Those theories, in turn, are partly related to the personalities of the counselors who developed them. The result of this is that any particular style of counseling is not equally effective for everyone. In fact, for any one person, the style that would work best at one point in his life may be different from what would work best at another time. You should also be aware that studies comparing styles of counseling have shown that effectiveness depends more on the personality and experience of the counselor, than on which style is used.

So why do we recommend the techniques in this book to all men who have been violent with a partner? This book offers you specific techniques that you can use to change the behavior of domestic violence. We, and other counselors, have found a combination of these techniques, and understanding the causes of violence, to be most effective in helping men to eliminate family violence from their lives. We recognize that each man has his own inner reasons and motives that give rise to the violence. While we encourage you to look deeply into yourself, a book cannot offer specific guidance for you, which is why we recommend individual or group counseling. *Learning to Live Without Violence* focuses on eliminating violence as a first step.

How to Look for What you Want

The following is a step-by-step approach to finding the best program or counselor for you.

Step 1: Contact a local domestic violence men's program

Programs that specialize in this problem are rapidly appearing in many parts of the country. These programs are usually run by men (and sometimes women) who have a good understanding of this problem. They have worked with many people and probably understand many of your particular needs. These programs are usually listed in the Yellow Pages under **Battered Women**, **Crisis Intervention Services** or **Social Service Agencies**. The police, or counseling agencies such as community mental health services, may know of such programs in your community. If you are unable to locate a specific domestic violence men's program in your area, proceed to step two.

Step 2: Contact a local battered women's shelter or program

Shelters or safe houses for battered women are places (usually a secret location) where women can find refuge from an abusive situation. These programs usually have a twenty-four hour hotline. Shelters are usually aware of reputable programs and individuals in their area that provide counseling to women and men. You may find their number by looking in the Yellow Pages under **Battered Women**, **Crisis Intervention Services** or **Social Service Agencies**. If these are not listed, look for other crisis hotlines like **Suicide Prevention**, **Child Abuse Hotline**, or **The United Way**. You may find out there is no battered women's shelter or program in your area. If this is so, proceed to the next step.

Step 3: Contact other crisis lines

The Yellow Pages has a listing called "**Crisis Intervention Services**." Under this listing you will find hotlines such as child abuse, suicide prevention, rape crisis and alcohol and drug lines. If there isn't a hotline for battered women and batterers, call one of the other hotlines. Their staff is usually aware of programs or therapists in their area that work well with specific problems. You don't need to give your name to the crisis worker, so don't be afraid to tell them that the problem is domestic violence. The more specific you are, the better able they will be to refer you to the appropriate agency or individual. If this approach doesn't work for you, proceed to step four.

Step 4: Contact other mental health professionals

Go back to the Yellow Pages and look up the following:

1. Marriage, Family and Child Counselor
2. Physicians (Psychiatrist)
3. Psychologist
4. Social Worker

Under each of these listings you'll find names of agencies and individuals. Agencies may have a variety of counselors for you to choose from, and may be appealing to a tight budget, because most agencies charge on a sliding scale. Many counselors in private practice charge on a sliding scale as well.

Pick out several names and give each one a call. You may want to talk with them over the phone or you may want to set up an appointment to meet with them in person. Try to be direct and tell them about the violence and your need to learn how to manage your anger differently. Feel free to ask them about their experience and counseling approach. In the front of this book (page viii) is a letter to whatever program or counselor you choose to see. The purpose of the letter is to help orient the counselor to our approach, and it may also be viewed as a letter of introduction for you. Xerox it and show it to your counselor, or read it to him or her over the phone.

A male or female counselor?

Is it important to you whether you see a man or woman counselor? We believe that it is much more important to look at a counselor's experience and qualifications than to choose on the basis of male or female. On the other hand, some men may feel uncomfortable talking to a woman about anger and violence, while other men may feel uncomfortable talking to a man. The choice here may depend on your personal preference. If in doubt, bring up this issue and discuss it directly with the counselor you interview.

Group, individual or couples counseling?

Men sometimes wonder whether they should attend group, individual or couples counseling. There are advantages to each. With group counseling, the main advantage is the opportunity to talk with and get support from other men who are experiencing this problem. In individual counseling, men are able to get more specialized attention, which enables them to focus on some underlying problems or issues. Once a man learns to control his anger and stop the violence, he needs to bring these skills into his relationship. We usually suggest couples counseling only after a man has first made these personal changes.

Length of counseling

How long should you go to counseling? Some programs for men are open-ended, which means you can stay as long as you want. Other programs may last for a specified period of time (such as 12, 16 or 24 weeks). If you are in such a short-term program you will want to speak with one of the counselors about continuing in individual, couples or group counseling after you complete the program. We have found that the men who have stayed in counseling the longest (at least two years) are less likely to commit additional violence. For a man and his family to be reasonably assured that his violence will stop, we recommend that he continue in some form of counseling for several years. This counseling may take different forms at different times. His first year may consist of group counseling followed by individual counseling. The second year may be a combination of individual and couples counseling. However, as we mentioned before, you need to take one day at a time; don't think about the end when you are just beginning.

How will you know when you are finished with counseling? No matter what a person's difficulty, whether it is alcohol, violence or other behavior problems, even if he is in counseling there is always the possibility that the behavior will recur. But when a man drops out of counseling before he is ready, he is likely to fall back into his old patterns. A man is ready to leave counseling when a number of people agree that he has sufficiently changed that violence is unlikely to reoccur. This decision should be made by the man, his partner, family members, and, of course, his counselor. As counselors, we feel comfortable that a man has reached this point when he has demonstrated a comfort in expressing his feelings, when he is conscious of the "old baggage" he brings into the relationship, and how these issues affect his behavior with his partner and other family members. We like to see men responding to the problems they encounter in life from a position of high self-esteem, rather than as a victim. Men are less likely to need counseling when they can see in themselves their impulses to react, rather than respond, and can control those impulses. Men who can step outside themselves for the moment and can consciously choose to act in a way that is most healthy for themselves and their families, are less in need of counseling.

Even when everyone agrees that counseling could be terminated because the man has demonstrated these qualities, we suggest that he always consider himself at risk for violence. In this way he can continue to grow personally by choosing, every day, to take responsibility by working at changing his attitude and behavior.

We have found that when the violence stops in a relationship, other problems may surface — such as communication difficulties, power struggles, too much dependency, and possessiveness. These problems are often best solved in couples counseling. One of the mistakes that both men and women (and sometimes therapists!) make is to attempt couples counseling too soon. In order for couples counseling to work, the violence has to have stopped. And to do that, the man must take personal responsibility. This gives the man the power to take the first step towards a positive new relationship.

In reading the newspapers and watching the television, one becomes aware of how many "family disputes" or "lovers quarrels" end in death. Like most other problems, we usually think it happens only to other people. But it **can** happen to you. This is why we say **stop the violence first**, then work on the underlying problems that may contribute to the source of conflict.

It's important for you to feel good about the counselor you see. Trust your intuition. If you don't feel comfortable with him or her, chances are you'll avoid going.

Alcohol and Drug Use

Men who abstain from **all** chemicals during their counseling are in a much better position to stop their violence and learn new ways to manage their anger and other feelings. As you use *Learning to Live Without Violence* we hope you will become more aware of your feelings — especially the ones that are easy to stuff and ignore — and communicate them more directly. Mood-altering chemicals counteract that awareness. They numb your feelings and make it easier to stuff them, or they make it more dangerous to express your feelings, since you have less conscious control. If your don't habitually use chemicals, making the commitment to stop for a short time will not be difficult. If you can't stop — or choose not to — you may have a problem.

Family and Friends

As you probably can tell, we're sold on the value of counseling to help you eliminate violence and live a more satisfying life. However, there is one important resource that you don't have to look up in the Yellow Pages — your family and friends.

110

As part of our upbringing, men are taught to expect to handle problems ourselves, without asking for help. This often leaves us feeling isolated when things go wrong, even from those who are closest to us. This isolation, and the pressure of being more self-sufficient than is humanly possible, can cause severe stress. And the more "on edge" you are, the more you're likely to blow up at a moment's notice.

This is why we encourage men in our program to talk to their families, and to other men, about the problems they are having at home. Start with the people who **you know** care about you. Your family may be able to give support and understanding, no matter what the situation. Many men in our groups have told us that friends are especially important. They can often listen objectively where a family member might tend to be judgmental. Men often describe how hard it was to **begin** to discuss these problems with a friend — and then it turned out that their friend had been having similar problems! We have found that friends are likely to be more understanding than you might expect — if you can discuss your problems frankly.

If there is no one to whom you can turn, finding a counselor you can trust is even more essential. You may want to begin thinking of ways to build closer friendships in the future. Your counselor will be able to help you develop plans for finding friends and decreasing your sense of isolation.

Utilizing Your Daily Program

Some men come into our program wanting a guarantee that we can help them stop battering for the rest of their lives. Others feel the pressure that if they batter again, their family will fall apart, or they will go to jail. They feel as though they are walking on eggs. How can they stop a lifelong pattern immediately? We answer them, "...by taking one day at a time." This is all you can do. Every day you have to wake up and do the best you can do to stop your violence. You need a plan just for that day. For example:

> "Today I am going to take one practice Time-Out, at least one real Time-Out, and tonight I am going to sit down with my wife and express my feelings about the abuse I experienced as a child."

That is quite a lot to do in one day, but this person is making a concerted effort to change his behavior, and that is what it takes, work! Often, men just forget about their anger and violence when they are not in their group, counseling or in court. However, recovering from domestic violence requires a daily effort. It requires a daily plan of action. You may decide when you wake up that you want to focus on one of the issues discussed in this book. For example:

> "Today, I want to focus on how my jealousy gets in the way of our relationship."

or

> "Today, I am going to be sensitive to ways I try to control and dominate my wife."

Make a plan for today. What can you do in the next twenty-four hours to change your pattern of anger and violence?

1._____

2._____

3._____

4._____

Study Questions

1. What type of counseling would you benefit from?

2. What qualities are important in a counselor?

3. What are the advantages of counseling? Describe your experiences with counseling in the past.

4. What counseling resources do you know of in your community?

5. What is your plan of action now that you have finished this book, group, program, etc.?

6. What steps do you plan to take to stay violence-free?

A LAST WORD

We hope that you are satisfied with where you have arrived with the help of this book. If you're like most men, some areas were easier for you to master than others. We encourage you to go back and re-read the more difficult chapters and repeat the exercises. You may find that you need to repeat a chapter several times before you get the full benefit of its information. Take your time, practice the exercises, and be sure that you have incorporated the new skills into your own behavior.

An important step in the recovery process is to talk with family and friends about your problem with violence. The purpose of this is not to "confess your sins" or to punish yourself; instead, the purpose is to let them know you are working on your problems and would like their support and assistance. You may discover that other family members or friends also have this problem. We recommend that you let them know about this book, and that counseling is available to solve this problem. One way of helping yourself is to help others.

As you talk about your own violence, you are likely to remember past incidents of violence from your childhood. You may find yourself feeling very angry at one or both of your parents. If you were abused, or saw your mother or father being abused, a necessary step in your own healing process will be to face the feelings you carry as a result of that violence. This may or may not include confronting your parents, or other persons who abused you. However, it will be very helpful for you to resolve these issues from the past with a qualified counselor, so that they do not have a negative influence on how you live your life today.

One final suggestion: Pick up this workbook again after a few months. Review the chapters to see how they may still apply to you, and to see also how your viewpoint has changed.

Good luck!

APPENDIX

STARTING A SELF-HELP PROGRAM

At the time of this writing, there are only a handful of self-help groups for men who batter, across the country. This is in part related to the fact that few men who batter readily acknowledge their urgent need for counseling and support. In addition, a man usually feels embarrassment and shame for having beaten his partner. These feelings get in the way of standing up in his community and identifying himself as a man who has battered. The community as a whole may still deny the seriousness and prevalence of domestic violence.

In spite of these facts, there are men who want to form self-help groups, and there continues to be a need for these groups all across the country. How can you get such a group off the ground?

Some self-help groups have started with a group of men who have all attended a domestic violence men's group together. They have graduated at about the same time and decided to start meeting on their own. They are likely to utilize the same format as the group they have come from. They may also use a book such as this to guide them in the structure of their meetings. Some self-help domestic violence groups are using the Alcoholics Anonymous Twelve Step program to structure their group meetings. Once you have your meetings on a regular basis, more people will get to know about them, and new members will find their way into the group.

Many self-help groups ask members for donations to pay for expenses for the meetings such as rent, refreshments, advertising, etc. Your group could similarly ask for donations from the members. This money could also be used for advertisement in local newspapers, production of fliers, mailing expenses and other expenses. If you are a self-help group, and are non-profit, you may be able to get certain items donated, such as a meeting space and some forms of advertisement, and publicity.

Another means of reaching out to the public is through a speakers' bureau. Members of your group could speak about the problem of family violence to local organizations (Rotary, Chamber of Commerce, etc.), churches, schools, mental health agencies, shelters for battered women and employee assistance programs. When radio and television find out about your self-help group they may want to interview some of your members. The media is an excellent way to reach many potential members, at no cost! Several years ago we advertised for our group with several public service announcements:

Christmas/Hanukkah

Holiday expectations of family closeness and good cheer can lead to disappointment, conflict and sometimes domestic violence. For one alternative to violence call **LEARNING TO LIVE WITHOUT VIOLENCE** at 555-1234.

```
┌─────────────────────────────────────────────────────────────┐
│                       NEW YEARS                             │
│                                                             │
│   You can get closer to the ones you love in the coming year │
│  by learning new ways of communicating anger, and solving   │
│  family problems without violence. You can learn to live    │
│  without violence. For help call LEARNING TO LIVE           │
│  WITHOUT VIOLENCE at 555-1234.                              │
└─────────────────────────────────────────────────────────────┘
```

```
┌─────────────────────────────────────────────────────────────┐
│   Domestic violence affects one in four families. Make a    │
│  New Year's resolution to learn new ways of handling anger, │
│  stress and conflict at home. For help call LEARNING TO     │
│  LIVE WITHOUT VIOLENCE at 555-1234.                         │
└─────────────────────────────────────────────────────────────┘
```

```
┌─────────────────────────────────────────────────────────────┐
│                    SUPERBOWL  SUNDAY                         │
│                                                             │
│   Family problems? Unnecessary roughness at home only causes│
│  more problems. Instead, take a Time-Out! For help learning │
│  non-violent ways of tackling anger, conflict and           │
│  disagreement, call LEARNING TO LIVE WITHOUT VIOLENCE       │
│  at 555-1234.                                               │
└─────────────────────────────────────────────────────────────┘
```

What do you do at the first meeting?

If you are meeting with a group of men from your counseling or education program, you may decide to use a format similar to what was used in that program. You may also want to utilize the material in this book. In either case, it is important that you clarify your group rules. In order for the group to run smoothly, it is necessary that the members are clear about what to expect of one another. For example, you may want to use the following group rules about how men will share in the group:

- Do not interrupt when people are talking

- No advice giving — talk about your feelings

- Start on time

- End on time

- No touching without permission from others

- No alcohol or drugs 24 hours before group

- No eating or drinking during sessions

- Keep the focus of conversation on anger and violence (or the chapter of the week)

- Keep to the structure of the group

- Decide on a facilitator ahead of time

- Honesty

It is also important for men to know that what is discussed in the group is confidential. That means you should not even talk with your partner about something one of the men said in the group. You may want to talk to her about general issues, but in discussing specifics, you may inadvertently reveal a member's identity.

Like other self-help groups, you may want to elect officers, such as treasurer (responsible for collecting money, bank deposits, etc.), facilitator (leads group for that session or series), administrator (plans meetings, secures meeting space, etc.) and educator (plans speakers' bureau). You may eventually want to develop a crisis line and have members volunteer to be available for emergency and information calls. It is a major undertaking to develop a hot-line. You need money and trained staff. It may be a project to consider once you have your group already in progress. In the meantime, members could exchange numbers so that individuals in crisis have a person to contact between meetings. You may also want to assign new members a sponsor; that is, a more experienced member who is familiar with the program and the recovery process.

The Group Check-In

At the beginning of each group, each member needs to briefly discuss the highlights of their week. This is called the group check-in. It is completed by answering the questions below. In this way the group leaders or facilitators will know how each man in progressing in the program. After the check-in, persons who perpetrated violence in the past week, those who are having difficulty utilizing the anger management material, or those who are in crisis have the opportunity to discuss their situation and receive group support in changing their patterns.

Group Check-In

1. Did you perpetrate physical, sexual, property or psychological violence this week?

2. How many real Time-Outs did you take this week?

3. How many practice Time-Outs did you take this week?

4. How many times did you get angry when you might have taken a Time-Out, but didn't? What did you do instead?

5. Are there any important issues you need to discuss in the session today?

After the group check-in, the men who perpetrated violence need to discuss their situation first. In doing so they should try to address the following questions:

Processing Acts of Violence

1. What violence did you perpetrate? What specifically did you do?

2. When did you notice you were becoming angry? How did you know you were angry?

3. When could you have chosen to act in another way? What might have been another way of dealing with the situation?

4. What is your plan of action for the next week? What can you do to lessen the chance of another incident of violence?

Having a plan of action is a good way to avoid another incident. This plan may include finding an individual counselor, attending AA or another chemical abuse program, separating, taking a Time-Out every day, reading and completing the exercises in a particular chapter in this book. Whatever the plan, it should involve specific, observable behaviors. Vague or general statements such as, "I'll try harder," or "I'll never do it again," or "I'll just stop it," are hard to hold to and don't set up markers for measuring improvement. Remember, stopping violence is an active, not passive process!

Men who are not taking Time-Outs are at high risk for future violence. They need to be encouraged to use this material even if they feel like their problem has gone away or they are getting along with their partner. Don't forget, every couple, no matter how good the relationship, argues. **If a man doesn't or can't take a Time-Out when he doesn't need one, he's not likely to take one when he does need one!**

When a man is in crisis, such as his wife leaving him, he will initially **just need to talk**. Let him! He needs to be **believed** about how much he hurts inside. Don't try to talk him out of his feelings ("Don't worry, you'll feel better tomorrow," or "You are better off this way"). Just accept how he feels and give him **support** ("I know what it's like," or "I understand that you are feeling bad"). You may not have anything to say and that is all right. You might want just to listen. Some men may need additional counseling. Chapter 13 in this book helps men find the right counselor.

Learning to Live Without Violence, is designed for use in brief, counselor-led educational groups and peer-led self-help groups. Contact a local bookstore and ask the manager to keep sufficient numbers of copies in stock for your program. You can also write directly to the publisher for group discount prices. This book contains all the information you will need to get your group off the ground. The rest will depend on your creativity and persistence.

In your attempt to get your group started, you may find programs in your area which are excellent resources. Battered women's shelters, Alcoholics Anonymous, and other self-help programs may be available to share their experience in developing their programs. Don't get isolated. Always let other programs know about your plans. Be willing to share and learn from others' experience. And most important of all, support each other's efforts.

SUGGESTED READING

Alcoholics Anonymous (1960). *Alcoholics anonymous*. New York: Alcoholics Anonymous World Services.

Bass, Ellen and Davis, Laura (1988). *The courage to heal: A guide for women survivors of child sexual abuse*. New York: Harper and Row.

Black, Claudia (1981). *It will never happen to me: Children of alcoholics as youngsters, adolescents and adults*. Denver, CO: M.A.C. Publications.

Bloom, Lynn; Cobern, Karen and Perlman, Joan (1975). *The new assertive woman*. New York: Dell.

Browne, Angela (1987). *When battered women kill*. New York: Free Press.

Butler, Sandra (1978). *Conspiracy of silence: The trauma of incest*. Volcano, CA: Volcano Press, (updated 1985).

Davis, Martha, Eshelman, Elizabeth Robbins, McKay, Matthew (1982). *The relaxation and stress reduction workbook*. Oakland, CA: New Harbinger Publications.

Dutton, Donald, G. (1988). *The domestic assault of women: Psychological and criminal justice perspectives*. Boston: Allyn and Bacon.

Ganley, Anne, L. (1981). *Court mandated counseling for men who batter (participants and trainers manuals)*. Washington, D.C.: Center for Womens Policy Studies.

Gilligan, Carol (1982). *In a different voice: Psychological theory and womens development*. Cambridge, MA : Harvard University Press.

Leonard, Linda (1983). *The wounded woman*. Athens, OH: Swallow Press.

Lerner, Harriet Goldhor (1985). *The dance of anger: A woman's guide to changing the patterns of intimate relationships*. New York: Harper and Row.

Levinson, Daniel (1978). *The seasons of a man's life*. New York: Ballantine Books.

Lew, Mike (1988). *Victims no longer: Men recovering from incest*. New York: Nevraumont Publishers.

Martin, Del (1976). *Battered wives*. Volcano, CA: Volcano Press, (rev. 1981).

Morris, Gregory (1985). *The kids next door: Sons and daughters who kill their parents*. New York: Morrow.

Porter, Eugene (1986). *Treating the young male victim of sexual assault*. Syracuse, NY: Safe Society Press.

Rubin, Lillian B. (1983). *Intimate strangers*. New York: Harper and Row.

Rubin, Lillian B. (1986). *Just friends: The role of friendship in our lives*. New York: Harper and Row.

Sonkin, Daniel; Martin, Del and Walker, Lenore (1985). *The male batterer: A treatment approach*. New York: Springer Publishing.

Sonkin, Daniel (1987). *Domestic violence on trial: Psychological and legal dimensions of family violence*. New York: Springer Publishing.

Sonkin, Daniel (1989). *The wounded man: Healing from childhood abuse*. San Francisco, CA: Harper and Row.

Walker, Lenore (1979). *The battered woman*. New York: Harper and Row.

Walker, Lenore (1984). *The battered woman syndrome*. New York: Springer Publishing.

Zilbergeld, Bernie (1978). *Male sexuality*. Boston: Little, Brown and Co.